David McCarter's
VB Tips and Techniques

DAVID McCARTER

apress™

David McCarter's VB Tips and Techniques
Copyright ©2000 by David McCarter

Developmental Editor: Nancy DelFavero
Page Composition: Impressions Book and Journal Services, Inc.
Indexer: Mike Gossman
Cover and Interior Design: Derek Yee Design

Distributed to the book trade worldwide by Springer-Verlag New York, Inc.
175 Fifth Avenue, New York, NY 10010
In the United States, phone 1-800-SPRINGER; orders@springer-ny.com
http://www.springer-ny.com

For information on translations, please contact APress directly:
APress, 6400 Hollis Street, Suite 9, Emeryville, CA 94608
Phone: 510/595-3110; Fax: 510/595-3122; info@apress.com; www.apress.com

Dedication

This book is dedicated to my children, Paul and Danielle.
They always inspire me to do my best and to be a good father.
Their undying love gets me through each and every day.

Acknowledgments

IT TOOK A NUMBER OF YEARS TO GET MY second book out and there are a lot of people to thank. I'd like to first thank all the readers and contributors of the *VB Tips & Tricks* newsletter. Without your support since 1993, the newsletter project and this book would have never seen the light of day. Thanks to all those who took the time to write e-mail letters of encouragement that kept me going, knowing that in some way I helped with your programming problems.

I'd like to thank Dan Appleman and Gary Cornell from Apress for giving me the opportunity to publish my second book, and the book's editor, Nancy DelFavero. I'd also like to thank (in no particular order) the following individuals for helping me during my Visual Basic programming career: Ted Torres, Robert Scoble, Matt Carter, Carl Franklin, Gary Wisniewski, Woody Pewitt, and all the guys who help me run the San Diego Visual Basic User Group. I'd also like to thank those who inspired me and helped me out from time to time: Alan Cooper, Dan Appleman, Deborah Kurata, Brad Kaenel, Carl Franklin, Phil Weber, and other fellow writers for the *Visual Basic Programmers Journal*. If I forgot anyone, it was not on purpose. There are many more who have helped and inspired me.

I'd also like to thank my students at the University of California, San Diego, for helping me to be a better teacher. Many of their ideas and questions made it into this book or on the VB Tips & Tricks Web site. I'd like to thank my coordinator at UCSD, Lee Graf, and Melanie Koellmann, for believing in me. I also need to include Michele Leroux Bustamante in this list for getting me into teaching in the first place.

Writing a book is not a very easy thing to do. It's very painstaking at times and takes over your life for a number of months. So, I'd like to give thanks to the following for helping me get through it all: Thanks to the makers of Dr. Pepper and Gatorade and Rock 105.3 radio station for helping me stay up at night to complete the book. Thanks to the makers of Line 6 guitar amplifiers, Gibson guitars, and Ibanez guitars for giving me the tools to work out the built-up stress. And thanks to all the members of DTBN (you know who you are) who helped me have some fun for a few hours from time to time . . . which helped me stay sane not only through this process but in general.

David McCarter
April 2000

About the Author

DAVID MCCARTER HAS BEEN A PROFESSIONAL programmer for over seven years. He also teaches Visual Basic programming at the University of California, San Diego. Since 1993 he has published a newsletter for Visual Basic programmers called *VB Tips & Tricks* (www.vbtt.com). David has been a contributing writer and technical editor for the *Visual Basic Programmers Journal*. His first book, *VB Tips and Tricks, Volume 1* (Mabry), was published in 1997. David also is on the steering committee of the San Diego Visual Basic Group.

Contents at a Glance

Contents

Chapter 4 Disk and File Tips and Tricks 39

Chapter 5 Tips and Tricks to Use with Forms 61

Chapter 9 Tips and Tricks on Some Advanced Stuff 133

Chapter 10 Miscellaneous but Nevertheless
Super-Useful Tips 147

Introduction

THIS BOOK IS MY SECOND THAT DEALS WITH various real-world programming challenges you'll face during your career. My first book on the subject, *VB Tips & Tricks,* Volume 1 (Mabry), included mostly tips for beginners, along with some tips for intermediate programmers.

This new book contains tips geared primarily to intermediate to advanced programmers, although it can be useful to programmers at any level of Visual Basic knowledge. (I've even included an opening chapter with tips for beginners that more-experienced programmers should also find valuable!)

How to Use This Book

This book is meant to be a handy technical reference for those times when you need special help with Visual Basic, or when you happen to find a Visual Basic bug. Although this book wasn't meant to be read from cover to cover in one sitting, I do recommend skimming the whole book to familiarize yourself with its contents. You can also browse the book's Contents or Index for help.

If you can't find a solution here, you can also search the VB Tips & Tricks Web Site (`www.vbtt.com`; see Appendix A for more information) or one of the other worthwhile Visual Basic information sources (see Appendix B for a listing).

How to Use the Tips in This Book

Every tip in this book has been fully tested and should work in most projects. Nevertheless, before you add code from a tip to your project, *save the project first!* All the tips for the 32-bit versions of Visual Basic were tested in Visual Basic 6.

The code you see under the "Declare" subheadings in each chapter should be placed in module files or in the general section of Forms and Classes, unless otherwise noted. The code under the "Code" subheadings should be placed wherever you think is appropriate for your application, unless otherwise noted. The code under the "Example" subheadings are demonstrations of how to use the code discussed in each tip.

Code Naming Conventions

All the tips in this book use the Microsoft Consulting Services Naming Conventions for Visual Basic. You can find an HTML file that describes these naming conventions in the answer to Q110264 on the Microsoft MSDN Web site.

The one rule I do not follow in the Microsoft naming conventions is the one regarding the prefix for Integers. The conventions call for using n as the prefix. For example:

```
Dim nCounter as Integer
```

I have in the past, and still to this day, use i as the prefix because i (for integer) is more mnemonic that n. For example:

```
Dim iCounter as Integer
```

Getting the Example Source Code

The code from the programming examples provided in this book may be downloaded from the Apress Web site. Just head to the page dedicated to this book:

```
www.apress.com/titles/1-893115-22-4
```

The sample code for each chapter is in a Zip file ready for downloading. Other programs and articles mentioned in this book will also be available from the site. Any "fixes" to the tips in this book will also be posted there.

Getting Updates to the Example Code

There are bound to be updates or corrections to the code in this book. Luckily, you can find them at either one of two places. The first is a special Web site created just for readers of this book. The URL for the site is `www.vbtt.com/vbttv2`. The second place is the Apress Web page devoted to this book.

Contacting the Author

You can contact David McCarter via Internet e-mail at davidm@vbtt.com. You can also visit his VB Tips & Tricks Web site at `www.vbtt.com`. See Appendix A for more information on the site.

CHAPTER 1

Some Hot Tips
to Get You Started

SOME OF THE OLDIES-BUT-GOODIES IN THIS CHAPTER will help you overcome problems that seasoned Visual Basic programmers can solve in their sleep (and I suspect they do), and some are just simple ways to work faster and better. You'll probably find yourself using these tips over and over again. Admittedly, these techniques are pretty basic, but they nevertheless serve as valuable reminders, and will get you ready to explore the rest of the book.

Setting Up the Visual Basic Design Environment

Compatible with: All 32-bit Versions of Visual Basic

Visual Basic has one of the best debugging environments around. It's so good other programming tools are starting to copy it. But, for some reason, Microsoft chose not to make the following settings the default. A big mistake! These settings can be found under the various tabs in the Tools ➜ Options dialog box.

Option Explicit Rules!

The following step is the very first thing you should do after installing Visual Basic. At the top of each file in your project, be sure to enter the following statement:

```
Option Explicit
```

In essence, this statement ensures that all of your variables in the file have been properly declared. Then, the Visual Basic debugger can find those variables and force you to declare them. Not only is this a good thing, but it also helps to point out variables that you may have misspelled.

So that you don't forget this very important step, select Require Variable Declaration under the Editor tab (see Figure 1.1). By default, all the Editor options are selected except that one. Visual Basic will add the Option Explicit statement to every *new* file you create in your project.

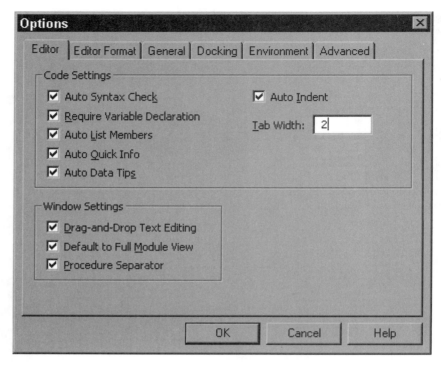

Figure 1.1. Don't forget to select the Require Variable Declaration option.

While you are at it, I recommend changing the Tab Width to 2 instead of the default 4. This just gives you more room on screen to view your code.

Compiling during Design Time

The second thing you should set up after installing Visual Basic is found under the General tab. Deselect the Compile On Demand check box (see Figure 1.2). For most projects, you want to leave it unchecked because Visual Basic does not compile your code or do any debugging until the code is called. Therefore, problems won't show up until the code is compiled, which makes those problems much harder to correct while you are running and testing your code.

Control Debugging

When you use the `On Error` statement to add an error trap to Visual Basic code, the effects may surprise you when running programs in the development environment. These effects are controlled under the General tab. For example, if you have the Break on All Errors box checked, the `On Error` statement will have no

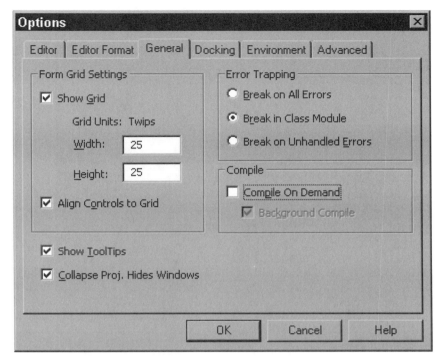

Figure 1.2. My advice is to Deselect the Compile on Demand option.

effect. You should instead have the Break On Unhandled Errors option checked when testing, and the Break In Class Module option checked when debugging code that uses class modules.

Using IntelliSense

Intellisense is the Microsoft "prompting" technology that helps you with the syntax for statements (it is available with Visual Basic 5 and 6). If you have Intellisense turned off, it is still available to you from the context menu that pops up when you right-click in the Code window. You can also use the context menu to get information without having to type the "=" sign or press the space bar to activate Intellisense.

Press Ctrl+J while you are in the edit window to quickly bring up the properties and methods window. While you are in a statement, you can press Ctrl+I to list the quick information for that statement. The popup lists all the parameters for the statement, the parameters data types (including default values if any), and puts "[and]" around parameters if they are optional.

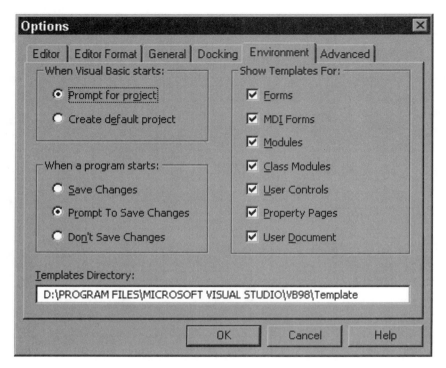

Figure 1.3. Make it a point to always select Prompt To Save Changes.

Saving Your Code Early and Often

This may seem almost too basic to even mention, but I'm going to make my speech anyway. If Visual Basic crashes because of a bad API call, a bad call to an object, or some other mishap, you'll lose a minimal amount of code if you remember to routinely save your code.

When setting up your Visual Basic environment, select Tools → Options and click the Environment tab. In that dialog box, select Prompt To Save Changes (see Figure 1.3). This option tells Visual Basic to ask you to save changes every time you run your project.

Making a Backup of a Project

Although you should always save your work using the method described in the previous tip, Visual Basic provides no quick way to back up a project. If you just choose the Save Project As option, you're merely creating a new Project file that lists the original parts of the project.

To make a backup of a project, you must save each individual piece of the project using a new name or in a new location. To accomplish the latter, it is usually easier to simply use Windows Explorer.

> **NOTE** *It is possible to write a Visual Basic add-in to do this automatically, and the upcoming Apress book,* Visual Basic Add-ins and Wizards *by Gary Cornell and David Jezak will show you how.*

Dealing with Docking and Other IDE Problems

The Visual Basic IDE is generally excellent, but Windows has an annoying habit of docking in the MDI (default *multiple document interface*) environment. To prevent a window from docking while you're moving it, hold down the Ctrl key while clicking and dragging. You can also use the Docking tab to make global changes to the way docking works.

If your development environment has become so jumbled that you long for the default positions of all the windows, the solution unfortunately requires using the RegEdit program to delete a key.

You need to completely delete the UI and Docking keys that may be found under

```
HKEY_CURRENT_USER\Software\Microsoft\Visual Basic\6.0
```

The next time you start up Visual Basic, the default behavior of all the windows in the Visual Basic environment will be restored.

> **WARNING** *This solution should not be attempted by an inexperienced user, or by any user who hasn't first made a backup of the registry.*

Building a Project from Form Files or Other Code Files

Occasionally, you may have only Form and code files but no Project file (a .vbp file), or you may find that the Project file is corrupted. Visual Basic will re-create a Project file for you if you follow these steps:

1. Start up a new project.

2. Remove the startup Form.

3. Add the Form files, class files, and code modules one by one to the project.

4. In the Project Properties dialog box, choose the desired startup object.

5. Save the project.

Visual Basic now recreates a project (.vbp file) for you.

Deleting Multiple Items in a ComboBox and ListBox

Compatible with: All Versions of Visual Basic
Applies to: ComboBox, ListBox

Deleting items out of a ComboBox or ListBox is easier than you might think. Just loop through all items and if an item in question is selected, just delete it! The trick here is to loop through the items backwards. If you were to go forward, when you delete an item, it would throw off the ListCount and eventually cause an error.

```
Private Sub Command1_Click()
Dim iCount As Integer
  For iCount = List1.ListCount - 1 To 0 Step -1
    If List1.Selected(iCount) Then
    List1.RemoveItem iCount
  End If
  Next iCount
End Sub
```

Adding Cut, Copy, Paste, and Undo Features Quickly

Compatible with: All Versions of Visual Basic
Applies to: Controls

The following is an easy way to put cut, copy, paste, and undo features into your program by using SendKeys.

```
Sub mnuEditText_Click(Index As Integer)
  Select Case Index
    Case 0 ' UNDO was chosen
      SendKeys "^Z"        ' Keys Ctrl+Z
```

```
    Case 1 ' CUT was chosen
      SendKeys "^X"          ' Keys Ctrl+X
    Case 2 ' COPY was chosen
      SendKeys "^C"          ' Keys Ctrl+C
    Case 3 ' PASTE was chosen
      SendKeys "^V"          ' Keys Ctrl+V
  End Select
End Sub
```

For greater control over the undo operation than what SendKeys provides, you can use the SendMessage API call. For more details on this, see Chapter 6.

Moving Files without All the Work

Compatible with: All Versions of Visual Basic
Applies to: Files

To move a file from one directory on a disk to another directory *on the same disk,* just use the Name function. This function is intended for renaming files, but it can also be used to move them. The following is sample code that demonstrates this:

```
Name "C:\MYTEXT.TXT" As "C:\SAVEDOCS\MYTEXT.TXT"
```

> **NOTE** *Wildcards are not permitted.*

Of course, before you execute this code, you must make sure that the destination directory exits. Here is how you can do that:

```
If Len(Dir("C:\SAVEDOCS", vbDirectory)) <> 0 Then
  Name "C:\MYTEXT.TXT" As "C:\SAVEDOCS\MYTEXT.TXT"
End If
```

CHAPTER 2

Tips on Working with Strings and Arrays

IN THIS CHAPTER, YOU'LL FIND TIPS ON DEALING with strings and arrays, including a few tips that introduce you to some of the new Visual Basic 6 string handling functions. These functions can make your programs run much cleaner and faster because you no longer have to write a bunch of code in order to manipulate strings!

Returning an Array of Fixed Length Strings

Compatible with: Visual Basic 6
Applies to: Arrays

At times, you may need to parse a string of fixed-length elements. For instance, you might have information returned from an instrument that sends ASCII data in a string such as -0.0001+0.0032-0.0012-0.0021, or a Web site that sends information in encoded form. The following little function will nicely chop up the string into fixed-length chunks, and return them as an array for further processing.

> **NOTE**   *This tip takes advantage of a new Visual Basic 6 feature that allows arrays to be passed back as the return of a function. This could not be done before Visual Basic 6.*

Code

Here is the code for the ParseFixedLenArray function.

```
Public Function ParseFixedLenArray(Work As String, _
                                   Length As Integer) _
                                   As String()

Dim aWork() As String
Dim lStartPos As Long
```

```
Dim lCounter As Long
  lStartPos = 1
  ReDim aWork(Len(Work) / Length)
  For lCounter = LBound(aWork) To UBound(aWork)
    aWork(lCounter) = Mid$(Work, lStartPos, Length)
    lStartPos = lStartPos + Length
  Next
  ParseFixedLenArray = aWork
End Function
```

Example

The following example shows you how to use the `ParseFixedLenArray` function.

```
Dim aData() As String
Dim sData As String
  sData = "-0.0001+0.0032-0.0012-0.0021"
  aData = ParseFixedLenArray(sData, 7)
```

Avoiding "Array Locked" Errors

Compatible with: Visual Basic 32-bit
Applies to: Arrays

Beware of exiting from a `With` block statement without tripping into the `End With` statement. This oversight can cause a `This array is fixed or temporarily locked` (Error 10) error when running your project. You'll get this error the second time you try to issue the `ReDim` statement on an array from which you've exited from inside a loop or procedure.

Example

The following example will reproduce the error I just described.

```
Private Type Student
  Name As String
  EMail As String
  GPA As String
End Type
Private Sub Command1_Click()
Dim aStudents() As Student
```

```
Dim lCounter As Long
  ReDim aStudents(1)
  For lCounter = LBound(aStudents) To UBound(aStudents)
    With aStudents(lCounter)
      If Len(.Name) = 0 Then
        'This will cause the error below
        Exit For
      End If
    End With
  Next
  'Error happens here
  ReDim aStudents(3)
End Sub
```

The solution is to restructure your code to always trip into the End With statement so Visual Basic will release the lock on the array.

New Visual Basic 6 String/Array Features

Compatible with: Visual Basic 6
Applies to: String, Arrays

I'll admit that this tip might seem like a given to some of you, but I have seen a lot
of Visual Basic 6 code that does not take advantage of the new strings functions
introduced in this version. I suppose some programmers don't look to see what's
new in the latest version. The section that lists what is new with each version is
the first place I head when I get a beta copy of Visual Basic. Here, I cover some of
my favorite new string/array features and briefly explain how to use them.

Filter

This function takes a one-dimensional array and returns only those items in the
array that match a filter criterion. In other words, it enables you to identify those
array items that either do or do not contain a specific string. This makes it easy to
find what you want in a large array. Here is an example of this function in action.

```
Private Sub Command1_Click()
Dim aData(2) As String
Dim aReturn() As String
  aData(0) = "VB Tips & Tricks"
  aData(1) = "Carl & Garys VB Home Page"
  aData(2) = "The Development Exchange"
  aReturn = Filter(aData, "VB", True)
End Sub
```

11

The array that returns from the code I just listed contains the following values because only those two array elements contain the target string "VB".

```
VB Tips & Tricks
Carl & Garys VB Home Page
```

By changing the value of the third true/false parameter (called the Include parameter), Filter cannot only return those items in the array to be searched that contain the target string (Include = True, the default), it can return the array items that do not contain the string that you're searching for (Include = False).

InStrRev

This function is similar to InStr except that it starts at the end of the string instead of the beginning. This difference makes it much easier to find a file name when you are given the full path name. Here is an example of how to use InStrRev.

```
Private Sub Command1_Click()
Dim sFilePath As String
Dim sFile As String
Dim lPos As Long
  sFilePath = "E:\Volume2\SampleCode\Chap10\FormatDrive.vbp"
  lPos = InStrRev(sFilePath, "\")
  sFile = Mid$(sFilePath, lPos + 1, Len(sFilePath) - lPos)
  MsgBox "The file name is" & sFile
End Sub
```

The value of sFile that you would see is

```
FormatDrive.vbp
```

This process is much easier and faster than looping through the string in a search for the last backslash character!

Split

This is one of my favorite new functions. It can take a string and split it into a zero-based array based on a *single* delimiter. In fact, I have used this function in some of the code that appears in this book. The following example gives you an idea of how to use it.

```
Private Sub Command1_Click()
Dim sFilePath As String
Dim aData() As String
  sFilePath = "E:\Volume2\SampleCode\Chap10\FormatDrive.vbp"
  aData = Split(sFilePath, "\")
End Sub
```

The previous code will return the following values in the `aData` array.

```
E:
Volume2
SampleCode
Chap10
FormatDrive.vbp
```

As you'll notice, you can easily parse the drive letter and file name from the string with just one line of code!

The `Split` function isn't perfect, however. Although it deals well with strings that contain a single delimiter, it doesn't work so well when you have multiple delimiters appearing together, or when you need to split on two different delimiters (such as "\" and "\\"). For instance, Split works great with strings such as "Thomas Alva Edison" but fails miserably on strings in which the user might have mistakenly added extra spaces, such as "Thomas   Alva   Edison".

The trick here is to first pass the string to a helper function that removes multiple copies of the delimiter while leaving only the one occurrence that `Split` can handle. I show you how to write this function using the nifty new `Replace` function in another tip that's coming up.

Join

This function is the opposite of `Split`. It takes an array and returns a single string. You can also define a delimiter to be placed between the array items. If you were to take the array from the `Split` example earlier and apply the following code to it (as you might do to make a local path for the Microsoft Information Server),

```
sFilePath = Join(aData, "\\")
```

the code would return the following line in the `sFilePath` variable:

```
E:\\Volume2\\SampleCode\\Chap10\\FormatDrive.vbp
```

Replace

This is another new String function I find myself using a lot. It will replace a substring in a string with another substring. Doing this replacement required many lines of code in older versions of Visual Basic. Now you can accomplish the same task with just one line of code and do it much faster! The following code provides an example of how to use Replace.

```
Private Sub Command1_Click()
Dim sName As String
  sName = "O'Brien"
  sName = Replace(sName, "'", "''")
End Sub
```

This code will return the following value for the sName variable:

```
O''Brien
```

The code can also be used to fix names before sending them to SQL queries (see Chapter 8 for a related tip).

So, how can you use Replace to turn the Split function into a "SuperSplit" function that can handle multiple delimiters (such as the extra spaces I mentioned earlier)? The idea here is to keep on calling Replace until there are no more multiple occurrences of the delimiter. The following shows you how the NoDoubleDelimiter function works.

```
Function NoDoubleDelimiters(sStuff As String, _
                            sDelim As String) As String
Dim sTemp As String
  sTemp = sStuff
  Do Until InStr(sTemp, sDelim & sDelim) = 0
    sTemp = Replace(sTemp, sDelim & sDelim, sDelim)
  Loop
  NoDoubleDelimiters = sTemp
End Function
```

The SuperSplit function merely has to call the NoDoubleDelimiters function before calling Split. The following is a version of a SuperSplit function. To make it more closely resemble the regular Split function, I allow the same optional parameters that you would have with the typical Split function.

```
Function SuperSplit(sStuff As String, _
                    Optional sDelim As String = " ",_
                    Optional Limit As Integer = -1, _
                    Optional Compare As _
                    VbCompareMethod = vbBinaryCompare) _
                    As String()
Dim sTemp As String
  sTemp = sStuff
  sTemp = NoDoubleDelimiters(sStuff, sDelim)
  SuperSplit = Split(sTemp, sDelim, Limit, Compare)
End Function
```

> **TIP**   *See Visual Basic help for all the information on these new features.*
> *Also check out "What's New in Visual Basic 6.0" in the Visual Basic help file*
> *to see a complete list of all the new features.*

CHAPTER 3
Tips on Working with Controls

THE TIPS AND TECHNIQUES IN THIS CHAPTER DEAL specifically with the standard controls that are included in the Visual Basic runtime DLL (dynamic-link library), and the OCX controls that ship with the Professional and Enterprise editions of Visual Basic. These tips can help you conquer those common problems we all face when we're adding controls to projects.

Using the Validate Event instead of LostFocus

Compatible with: Visual Basic 6
Applies to: All visible controls, except Line and Shape

The traditional method of validating information in a control such as a TextBox is to use code in the LostFocus event. The new Validate event has the advantage of being triggered *before* the control loses the focus.

To use the Validate event, simply set the CausesValidation property of the control to be True.

Verifying that TextBox Entries Are All Nonempty

Compatible with: All Versions of Visual Basic
Applies to: TextBox

Many programs use TextBox controls on a Form to enable the user to enter data. If the application requires every TextBox to be filled in, this tip provides an easy way to make sure data has been entered into all of them.

The following code loops through every TextBox on the Form (using For Each). If the TextBox is empty, the BackColor changes to pink (you may choose any color you want) and the function will return False. If data is entered in every TextBox, then the function will return True. It will also change any of the TextBox BackColor back to the Windows default (vbWindowBackground) if the color was changed to pink.

Code

You can use the following code to check that entries have been made in every TextBox.

```
Function IsTxtBoxesEmpty(Frm As Form) As Boolean
Dim ctlTestCtrl As Control
Const WARNING_COLOR = &HFFCOFF
  On Error Resume Next
  IsTxtBoxesEmpty = False
  'Loop through the controls
  For Each ctlTestCtrl In Frm.Controls
    If Trim$(ctlTestCtrl.Text) = vbNullString Then
      If Err.Number = 0 Then
        IsTxtBoxesEmpty = True
        'Change to Pink
        ctlTestCtrl.BackColor = WARNING_COLOR
      End If
      Err.Clear
      Else
        'If the color was Pink, change it back
        If ctlTestCtrl.BackColor = WARNING_COLOR Then
          ctlTestCtrl.BackColor = vbWindowBackground
        End If
    End If
  Next ctlTestCtrl
End Function
```

Example

Here is an example of how to use the IsTxtBoxesEmpty function. Notice that I use Me instead of the Form name. I did that because if the Form name is ever changed, this code will still work.

```
Private Sub Update_Click()
  If IsTxtBoxesEmpty(Me) Then
    MsgBox "Some textboxes are still empty"
  End If
End Sub
```

Automatic Selection of Text

Compatible with: All Versions of Visual Basic
Applies to: TextBox, ComboBox

When the contents of a TextBox or ComboBox get the focus, a well-designed user interface highlights the text so that it's ready for immediate editing by the user. This code will highlight the text of the ActiveControl of the ActiveForm.

Code

The following subroutine works by creating a Form object by first dimensioning it, and then setting it to the ActiveForm. Next, it selects the text of the Form's ActiveControl starting at the left-most character at the end of the text.

```
Sub HighlightText()
Dim frmTemp As Form
  On Error Resume Next
  Set frmTemp = Screen.ActiveForm
  frmTemp.ActiveControl.SelStart = 0
  frmTemp.ActiveControl.SelLength = Len(frmTemp.ActiveControl)
  Set frmTemp = Nothing
End Sub
```

You can use this subroutine in the GotFocus method of any control, such as a TextBox or a ComboBox, that allows text entry.

Example

Here's an example of how you would use the HighlightText subroutine in a GotFocus event of a control.

```
Private Sub Text1_GotFocus ()
   Call HighlightText
End Sub
```

Keeping Text Highlighted When the Focus Moves Away from a Control

Applies to: TextBox, RichTextBox, ListView, TreeView

A professionally designed program always keeps a control's text highlighted when the user moves away from the control to a Command Button, for instance. This highlighting can be maintained by changing the default value of the HideSelection property from True to False.

Ignoring Keyboard Characters in a TextBox Control

Compatible with: All Versions of Visual Basic
Applies to: TextBox

If you need to ignore certain ASCII characters in a TextBox, I know of a very easy way to accomplish that.

Example

The following code, when written in an event, will allow you to ignore keyboard characters of your choosing by setting a variable called sTemplate appropriately.

```
Private Sub Text1_KeyPress(KeyAscii As Integer)
Dim sTemplate As String
  sTemplate = "!@#$%^&*()_+-="
  If InStr(1, sTemplate, Chr(KeyAscii)) > 0 Then
    KeyAscii = 0
  End If
End Sub
```

Using a TextBox Control to Get the Effect of a Scrolling Form

Compatible with: Visual Basic 32-bit
Applies to: Form, RichTextBox

Although it is possible to use a PictureBox to give the appearance of a "scrolling Form" (see "Viewing an Oversized Picture Using Scroll Bars" later in this chapter), the extra code needed for this slick effect can be overkill. If all you want is a way to make a Form appear to scroll for large amounts of text, use the following steps.

1. Add a TextBox (or RichTextBox) to the Form with the Name property set to txtStuff, for example.

2. Set the Multiline property to be True.

3. Add Vertical Scroll bars.

4. Set the BorderStyle property to be 0-None.

5. Add the following code in the Form_Load.

    ```
    Private Sub Form_Load()
      txtStuff.BackColor = Me.BackColor
    End Sub
    ```

6. Now, add the following line of code to the Resize event.

    ```
    txtStuff.Move 0, 0, Me.ScaleWidth, Me.ScaleHeight
    ```

The result is a TextBox that completely fills the useable area. Because the background color has been adjusted, the TextBox gives the appearance of a scrolling Form for text.

Turning Off Word Wrap in a RichTextBox Control

Compatible with: Visual Basic 32-bit
Applies to: RichTextBox

For some reason, when Microsoft created the RichTextBox OCX (richtx32.ocx), they did not provide a word wrap (MultiLine) property such as the normal Visual Basic TextBox control has. If you want the RichTextBox to word wrap, just set the RightMargin of the RichTextBox to a large number, such as 100,000 or higher.

Adding the Default Context Menu to a RichTextBox

By default, the RichTextBox does *not* show the typical context-sensitive menu with the Cut/Paste/Undo options, for example, when right-clicking it. You can make this menu appear by setting the AutoVerbMenu property of the control to be True at both design time and runtime.

Using a RichTextBox to Add a Quick Save/Load File Capability

Compatible with: Visual Basic 32-bit
Applies to: RichTextBox

One of the niftiest (but perhaps underutilized) features of a RichTextBox is its ability to save its contents to a file in *either* rich text or ordinary text format. The syntax for this follows, where `FileType` is one of the constants `rtfRTF` or `rtfText`:

```
ControlName.SaveFile Pathname, FileType
```

Similarly, the syntax for `LoadFile` is this:

```
ControlName.LoadFile Pathname, FileType
```

At design time, you can add the contents of a file simply by setting the `Filename` property.

Toggling ListView Sorting Order Like You Can with Explorer

Compatible with: Visual Basic 32-bit
Applies to: ListView Control

The following code will sort a ListView control (part of the Microsoft Windows Common Controls OCX; mscomctl.ocx) column to be alternately ascending or descending on each subsequent mouse click. This feature works only in the Report View mode.

Code

This following code sorts the ListView list of items in ascending or descending order. Just copy and paste it into the `ColumnClick` event of any ListView control for which you want to implement this feature.

```
Private Sub ListView1_ColumnClick(ByVal ColumnHeader As _
                                  ColumnHeader)
Dim iSortKey As Integer
Static iLastSortOrder As Integer
Static iLastSortKey As Integer
Static bIsClicked As Boolean
  iSortKey = ColumnHeader.Index - 1
  'If same column, but not first time clicked...
```

```
  If (iSortKey = iLastSortKey) And bIsClicked Then
    'Toggle sort order
    iLastSortOrder = iLastSortOrder Xor lvwDescending
  Else
    'Different column, or first time here
    iLastSortOrder = lvwAscending
  End If
  With ListView1
    .SortOrder = iLastSortOrder
    .SortKey = iSortKey
    .Sorted = True
  End With
  'Set flag to say we've been
  bIsClicked = True
  'Save sorted column
  iLastSortKey = iSortKey
End Sub
```

Removing Selected Items from a ListView Control

Compatible with: Visual Basic 32-bit
Applies to: ListView control

You can remove every selected item from a ListView control fairly simply. With the code that follows, use the `ListViewSelected` function to determine if any items are selected in the control. If any items are selected, loop through the control and keep deleting items until the `ListViewSelected` function returns `False`.

　　To keep this code very fast and efficient, I am using the `SendMessage` API call to retrieve the information I need from the ListView control.

Declare

Put the following code in the Declarations section of a module file.

```
Private Const LVM_FIRST = &H1000
Private Const LVM_GETSELECTEDCOUNT = (LVM_FIRST + 50)
Public Const LVM_DELETEITEM = (LVM_FIRST + 8)
Public Const LVM_GETITEMCOUNT = (LVM_FIRST + 4)
Public Const LVM_GETITEMSTATE = (LVM_FIRST + 44)
Private Declare Function SendMessage Lib "user32" Alias _
        "SendMessageA" (ByVal hwnd As Long, ByVal wMsg As Long, _
        ByVal wParam As Long, lParam As Any) As Long
```

Code

The following subroutine will remove all selected items from the ListView control.

> **NOTE** *A couple interesting things are worth mentioning here: Whenever items need to be removed from a ListView or ListBox control, you need to loop through the control backwards so that the index number positioning does not get out of whack after the items are deleted. In addition, to check a ListView Item to see if it's selected, use the* SendMessage *API call with the* LVM_GETITEMSTATE *constant as the* wMsg *parameter and the* LVIS_SELECTED *constant as the* lParam *parameter.*

```
Sub RemoveLVSelectedItems(lvControl As MSComctlLib.ListView)
Dim lReturn As Long
Dim lCounter As Long
Dim lItemCount As Long
Dim lState As Long
  'Get the number of items in the ListView control
  lItemCount = SendMessage(lvControl.hwnd, LVM_GETITEMCOUNT, _
                             0, 0)
  For lCounter = lItemCount To 0 Step -1
    'Get the state of the item
    lState = SendMessage(lvControl.hwnd, LVM_GETITEMSTATE, _
                           lCounter, LVIS_SELECTED)
    'If it's selected, delete it!
    If lState = LVIS_SELECTED Then
      lReturn = SendMessage(lvControl.hwnd, LVM_DELETEITEM, _
                             lCounter, 0)
    End If
    'Get out of there are no more selected
    If ListViewSelectedCount(lvControl) = 0 Then
      Exit For
    End If
  Next
End Sub
```

This is the same function listed earlier in this chapter in the section "Getting the Number of Items Selected in a ListView Control."

```
Function ListViewSelectedCount(lvControl As MSComctlLib.ListView) As Long
Dim lReturn As Long
  lReturn = SendMessage(lvControl.hwnd, LVM_GETSELECTEDCOUNT, _
```

```
                          0, 0)
   ListViewSelectedCount = lReturn
End Function
```

Example

Here is an example of how to use the RemoveLVSelectedItems subroutine.

```
RemoveLVSelectedItems lstvSomeData
```

The sample code for this tip can be found in the ListView.vbp project in the Chapter 3 directory in the source code download (see the Introduction in this book for more information).

Getting the Number of Items Selected in a ListView Control

Compatible with: Visual Basic 32-bit
Applies to: ListView Control

In my projects, I use the ListView control as a souped-up list box. Oftentimes, I need to know the number of items selected in my code. Because the developers who wrote the ListView control at Microsoft apparently thought this would not be a good method to provide to us programmers, I wrote one of my own. It uses the SendMessage API call to get the selected count.

Declare

```
Private Const LVM_FIRST = &H1000
Private Const LVM_GETSELECTEDCOUNT = (LVM_FIRST + 50)
Private Declare Function SendMessage Lib "user32" Alias _
        "SendMessageA" (ByVal hwnd As Long, ByVal wMsg As Long, _
        ByVal wParam As Long, lParam As Any) As Long
```

Code

Here's the custom code I wrote to determine the number of selected items.

```
Function ListViewSelectedCount(lvControl As MSComctlLib.ListView) As Long
Dim lReturn As Long
```

```
    lReturn = SendMessage(lvControl.hwnd, LVM_GETSELECTEDCOUNT, _
                          0, 0)
    ListViewSelectedCount = lReturn
End Function
```

Example

And, here's an example of how you would use this function in your own code whenever you need to find out if any items are selected.

```
If ListViewSelectedCount(frmMain.lstvSingle) > 0 Then
    'Your Code Goes Here
End If
```

An example of this code can be found in the ListView.vbp project in the Chapter 3 directory on this book's companion source code download tree (see the Introduction in this book).

Grid Printing Made Easy

Compatible with: Visual Basic 6
Applies to: Microsoft FlexGrid Control

Would you like an easy way to print data from the Microsoft FlexGrid control that comes with Visual Basic 6? The following code prints a grid with all the necessary lines and makes the grid fit within the page width. It does this by decreasing the FontSize until the entire grid fits on the page. If the grid prints on multiple pages, the header and the page number are printed on each page of the grid.

Code

Although this code may not work for printing very complex reports, it will do just fine for simple ones. Just put this code in your project and go . . . it can't get any easier or faster than that!

```
Sub PrintFlexGrid(Grid As MSFlexGrid, Title As String, _
                  Lines As Boolean)
Dim lRow As Long
Dim lColumn As Long
Dim lCurrentX As Long
Dim lCurrentY As Long
Dim lMaxLine As Long
```

```
Dim iPage As Integer
Dim sPage As String
Dim lOldY As Long
Dim lPageWidth As Long
Dim lBeginLeft As Long
Dim lBeginGrid As Long
  If (Grid.Rows = 0) Then
    Exit Sub
  End If
 'Resize the grid
 GridSize Grid
 'Set Max Lines
 lMaxLine = 99999999
 'Set the fontsize of the grid
 Printer.FontSize = Grid.FontSize
 'Set the maximum width of the page
 lPageWidth = Printer.Width * 0.94 - 200
 'Calculate the maximum possible fontsize
 Do While (lMaxLine > lPageWidth) And (Printer.FontSize > 0)
   lMaxLine = 0
   For lColumn = 0 To Grid.Cols - 1
     lMaxLine = lMaxLine + (Printer.FontSize / Grid.FontSize) _
       * Grid.ColWidth(lColumn)
   Next
   'Change the fontsize if needed
   If (lMaxLine > lPageWidth) Then
     Printer.FontSize = Printer.FontSize - 1
   End If
 Loop
 'Begin on page 1
 iPage = 1
 'Print headers and title
 GoSub PRINT_HEADERS
 For lRow = 1 To Grid.Rows - 1
   If (Lines = True) Then
     Printer.Line (lBeginLeft, lCurrentY)-(lMaxLine, lCurrentY)
   End If
   'Print on a new page if needed
   If (lCurrentY >= Printer.Height * 0.93 - _
        Printer.TextHeight("A")) Then
     If (Lines = True) Then
       'Bottom line
       Printer.Line (lBeginLeft, lCurrentY - 4 * _
```

```
                              Printer.TwipsPerPixelY)-(lMaxLine, lCurrentY - 4 * _
                              Printer.TwipsPerPixelY)
                          'Left line
                          Printer.Line (lBeginLeft, lBeginGrid)- _
                            (lBeginLeft, lCurrentY - 4 * Printer.TwipsPerPixelY)
                          'Right line
                          Printer.Line (lMaxLine, lBeginGrid)- _
                            (lMaxLine, lCurrentY - 4 * Printer.TwipsPerPixelY)
                      End If
                      Printer.NewPage
                      iPage = iPage + 1
                      'Print headers and title
                      GoSub PRINT_HEADERS
                  End If
                  lCurrentX = 4 * Printer.TwipsPerPixelX
                  For lColumn = 0 To Grid.Cols - 1
                      If (lColumn > 0) Then
                          lCurrentX = lCurrentX + _
                            (Printer.FontSize / Grid.FontSize) * _
                            Grid.ColWidth(lColumn - 1)
                          If Lines = True Then
                              Printer.Line (lCurrentX - 4 * Printer.TwipsPerPixelX, _
                                lBeginGrid)-(lCurrentX - 4 * Printer.TwipsPerPixelX, _
                                Printer.CurrentY + (Printer.TextHeight("A") / 2) - _
                                4 * Printer.TwipsPerPixelY)
                          End If
                      End If
                      'Print cell text
                      Grid.Col = lColumn
                      Grid.Row = lRow
                      Printer.CurrentX = lCurrentX
                      Printer.CurrentY = lCurrentY + _
                        (Printer.TextHeight("A") / 2)
                      Printer.Print Grid.Text
                  Next
                  lCurrentY = lCurrentY + (Printer.TextHeight("A") * 2)
              Next
              If (Lines = True) Then
                  'Bottom line
                  Printer.Line (lBeginLeft, lCurrentY - 4 * _
                    Printer.TwipsPerPixelY)-(lMaxLine, lCurrentY - 4 * _
                    Printer.TwipsPerPixelY)
                  'Left line
```

```
      Printer.Line (lBeginLeft, lBeginGrid)- _
        (lBeginLeft, lCurrentY - 4 * Printer.TwipsPerPixelY)
       'Right line
      Printer.Line (lMaxLine, lBeginGrid)- _
        (lMaxLine, lCurrentY - 4 * Printer.TwipsPerPixelY)
   End If
   Printer.EndDoc
   Exit Sub
PRINT_HEADERS:
   'Print the title
   lCurrentY = Printer.CurrentY
   Printer.FontBold = True
   Printer.Print Title
   Printer.FontBold = False
   Printer.Print vbNullString
   'We print the page number on the first line
   lOldY = Printer.CurrentY
   sPage = "Page " & CStr(iPage)
   Printer.FontItalic = True
   Printer.CurrentX = lPageWidth - Printer.TextWidth(sPage)
   Printer.CurrentY = lCurrentY
   Printer.Print sPage
   Printer.FontItalic = False
   Printer.CurrentY = lOldY
   'Print the grid
   Printer.CurrentY = Printer.CurrentY + _
     (Printer.TextHeight("A"))
   lCurrentY = Printer.CurrentY
   lBeginGrid = lCurrentY
   lBeginLeft = 0
   lCurrentX = 4 * Printer.TwipsPerPixelX
   'Print the header of each column
   If (Lines = True) Then
     Printer.Line (lBeginLeft, lCurrentY)-(lMaxLine, lCurrentY)
   End If
   Printer.Print
   lCurrentY = Printer.CurrentY + (Printer.TextHeight("A") / 2)

   For lColumn = 0 To Grid.Cols - 1
     If (lColumn > 0) Then
       lCurrentX = lCurrentX + (Printer.FontSize / Grid.FontSize) _
         * Grid.ColWidth(lColumn - 1)
     End If
```

```vbnet
                'Print cell text
            Grid.Col = lColumn
            Grid.Row = 0
            Printer.CurrentX = lCurrentX
            Printer.CurrentY = lCurrentY
            Printer.Print Grid.Text
        Next
        lCurrentY = lCurrentY + (Printer.TextHeight("A") * 1.5)
        Printer.Print
        If (Lines = True) Then
            Printer.Line (lBeginLeft, lCurrentY)-(lMaxLine, lCurrentY)
        End If
        Return
End Sub
Sub GridSize(Grid As MSFlexGrid)
Dim sTemp As String
Dim lColSize As Long
Dim lCounter As Long
Dim iaTemp() As Integer
Dim iRow As Integer
    ReDim iaTemp(Grid.Cols)
    For lCounter = 0 To Grid.Cols - 1
        For iRow = 0 To Grid.Rows - 1
            sTemp = GridGetText(Grid, iRow, lCounter)
            lColSize = IIf(Len(sTemp)<1, 1, Len(sTemp))
            If (iaTemp(lCounter)<lColSize) Then
                iaTemp(lCounter) = lColSize
            End If
        Next
    Next
    For lCounter = 0 To Grid.Cols - 1
        Grid.ColWidth(lCounter) = iaTemp(lCounter) * _
            Grid.FontSize * 14
    Next
End Sub
Function GridGetText(Grid As MSFlexGrid, ByVal Row As Long, _
                        ByVal Col As Long) As String
Dim lOldCol As Long
    lOldCol = Grid.Col
    Grid.Row = Row
    Grid.Col = Col
    GridGetText = Grid.Text
    Grid.Col = lOldCol
End Function
```

Example

Here is an example of how to use the `PrintFlexGrid` subroutine.

```
Private Sub Command1_Click()
  PrintFlexGrid MSFlexGrid1, "TEST Print", True
End Sub
```

You can find this code in the PrintGrid.vbp project in the Chapter 3 directory in the source code download available on the Apress Web site (see this book's Introduction for more details).

Clicking an Object Using the Windows API

Compatible with: Visual Basic 32-bit
Applies to: Controls

When creating an "add-on" program, or a program that interacts with another program, you might need to fire keyboard or mouse events in an object. That's very easy to do, provided you have a Window handle (hWnd) for that object. You can just use the code that follows.

Although this code will cause keyboard events, you can also use other constants such as `WM_MBUTTONUP` or `WM_NCLBUTTONDOWN` to cause mouse events. Use the API Viewer in Visual Basic to look up other messages that you can send to objects.

Declare

Put this code in the Declarations section of a module file.

```
Public Declare Function SendMessage Lib "user32" Alias _
  "SendMessageA" (ByVal hWnd As Long, ByVal wMsg As Long, _
  ByVal wParam As Long, lParam As Any) As Long
Public Declare Function SetFocus Lib "user32" _
  (ByVal hWnd As Long) As Long
Public Const WM_KEYUP = &H101
Public Const WM_KEYDOWN = &H100
Public Const VK_SPACE = &H20
```

Code

The following code will click an object based on its hWnd property.

```
Sub ClickOnObject(hWnd As Long)
Dim lReturn As Long
  lReturn = SetFocus(hWnd)
  lReturn = SendMessage(hWnd, WM_KEYDOWN, VK_SPACE, 0)
  lReturn = SendMessage(hWnd, WM_KEYUP, VK_SPACE, 0)
End Sub
```

You can find the code for this tip in the ClickObject.vbp project in the Chapter 3 folder that is downloadable from the Apress Web site.

Viewing an Oversized Picture Using Scroll Bars

Compatible with: Visual Basic 32-bit
Applies to: PictureBox

Your users may at times want to view a picture that's larger than the Form that contains it. You could use the Image control and set the Stretch property to True, but a better way to view the same picture involves using scroll bars (see Figure 3-1). It's pretty easy to do; just use the code and settings that follow. This example is also a good introduction to the BitBlt API Function that allows you manipulate graphics.

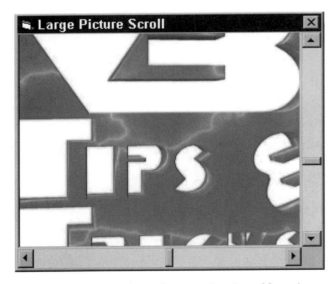

Figure 3-1. Oversized graphics can be viewed by using a single API call and two ScrollBars.

Declare

Put this code in the Declarations section of a module file.

```
Public Declare Function BitBlt Lib "gdi32" _
                        (ByVal hDestDC As Long, _
                              ByVal x As Long, _
                              ByVal y As Long, _
                              ByVal nWidth As Long, _
                              ByVal nHeight As Long, _
                              ByVal hSrcDC As Long, _
                              ByVal xSrc As Long, _
                              ByVal ySrc As Long, _
                              ByVal dwRop As Long) _
                              As Long
Public Const SRCCOPY = &HCC0020 ' (DWORD) dest = source
```

Setting Up the Form

First, you need to create the following four controls. Next, set their properties as listed with each control. ***Note:*** You must also set the Form's `ScaleMode` property to Pixel.

- Picture Box
    - Name = picSrc
    - AutoRedraw = TRUE
    - AutoSize = TRUE
    - Picture = (bitmap)
    - ScaleMode = 3 – Pixel
    - Visible = FALSE

- Vertical Scroll Bar
    - Name = vsVertical
    - Min = 0
    - Max = (leave at default value)

- Horizontal Scroll Bar
    - Name = hsHorzr
    - Min = 0
    - Max = (leave at default value)

- Picture Box
    - Name = picDest
    - ScaleMode = 3 - Pixel

Code

Add the following subroutine to your Form. It will do the work of scrolling your graphic.

```
Sub UpdatePic()
Dim lReturn As Long
  lReturn = BitBlt(picDest.hDC, 0, 0, picDest.Width, _
                picDest.Height, picSrc.hDC, _
                hsHorz.Value * ((picSrc.Width - picDest.Width) _
                / hsHorz.Max), vsVertical.Value * _
                ((picSrc.Height - picDest.Height) / _
                vsVertical.Max), SRCCOPY)
End Sub
```

Then, add the UpdatePic method to the following Events as shown.

```
Private Sub Form_Load()
  UpdatePic
End Sub
Private Sub Form_Resize()
  UpdatePic
End Sub
Private Sub hsHorz_Change()
  UpdatePic
End Sub
Private Sub hsHorz_Scroll()
  UpdatePic
End Sub
Private Sub picDest_Paint()
  UpdatePic
End Sub
Private Sub vsVertical_Change()
  UpdatePic
End Sub
Private Sub vsVertical_Scroll()
  UpdatePic
End Sub
```

Now your users can scroll a large graphic within a small form.

You can find this code in the LargePictureScroll.vbp project in the Chapter 3 directory that you can download from the Apress Web site.

Extending the Timer Control to Intervals beyond the 65.5-Second Range

Compatible with: All versions of Visual Basic

The Interval property of a Timer control typically can't be set to anything higher than 65,536 milliseconds (slightly more than 1 minute). To allow longer intervals, simply add a Static variable as follows. For example, to have code in a Timer that is activated every five minutes, first set the Interval property to 60,000 (one minute), and then use code such as this:

```
Sub Timer1_Timer()
Const MINUTES = 5
Static iNumOfMinutes As Integer
  iNumOfMinutes = iNumOfMinutes + 1
  If iNumOfMinutes Mod MINUTES <> 0 Then
    Exit Sub
  End If
  iNumOfMinutes = 0  'reset trigger
  'code you want to be triggered goes here
End Sub
```

Using the SysInfo Control to Determine When the Hardware Environment Changes

Compatible with: Visual Basic 32-bit

Although using specific API calls always adds a smaller memory requirement to your application, as compared with a control that encapsulates this information, controls often add specific event notification that API calls do not. For this reason, the SysInfo control (SYSINFO.OCX) that ships with the Professional and Enterprise versions is by far the easiest to be notified about changes in the user's environment.

For example, when the DisplayChanged event is triggered, the screen resolution was just changed, or when the SettingChanged event receives information, a system setting has changed (essentially capturing the WM_SETTINGCHANGED message).

Properties such as WorkAvailableArea, WorkAreaLeft, and WorkAreaTop are very useful because these properties return information concerning which part of the screen is safe to use. (For example, the user's TaskBar may have been moved to the top of the screen out of its normal location.)

This control is especially useful for programs running on laptops with PCMCIA cards that may be inserted or removed almost at will, in which case you need to be periodically updated on the status of the battery. For example, monitoring properties such as BatteryStatus or BatteryLifeTime can be crucial to your taking proper action if the battery is running low. Or, for instance, writing code in the DeviceArrival event lets you take advantage of a new device being added.

Using Windowless Controls to Make Properties Read/Write at Runtime

Compatible with: Visual Basic 6

Visual Basic ships with a set of "lightweight" controls you'll find in a file called MSWLESS.OCX. These controls are versions of the intrinsic controls, such as CommandButton and TextBox, that you see in the toolbox when you start up Visual Basic. The windowless versions work like the usual controls, with the following exceptions:

- They are much smaller and therefore can often be used advantageously when creating custom controls.

- These controls have no hWnd (window handle), so they can't be used with API calls.

- They cannot be containers for other controls.

Most properties for the intrinsic controls that are normally read-only at runtime are now read-write. This feature makes these ideal controls to be added dynamically at runtime via code (see the next tip).

Taking Advantage of Adding Controls Dynamically at Runtime

Compatible with: Visual Basic 6

Prior to Visual Basic 6, the only way to add controls at runtime was via a control array. This is no longer the case! You simply have to call the Add method of the Controls collection that's attached to a Form. The syntax for this is:

```
Set CtrlObjectName = FormName.Controls.Add ("ProgID", "key" [, ContainerName])
```

If you leave the parameter for the `ContainerName` off, the new control gets attached to the Form. The new controls must have their properties set to reasonable values before you can use them. The `ProgID` for intrinsic controls is `VB.ControlType.` For example,

```
Dim lblNewLabel As Label
  Set lblNewLabel = Form1.Controls.Add("VB.Label", "AReallyNewLabel")
```

For other controls, a good bet is that the ProgID begins with the name of the library you would see in the Object Browser if you added the control at design time, followed by a dot, followed by the name that shows up in the Properties Window.

To actually see the `Add` method in action, start up a new project and run the following `Form_Load`. By using the `WithEvents` keyword when you declare the control variable, you'll be able to make the new controls trigger events, just like controls added at design time.

Note how you need to set all the relevant properties for the new controls. Also notice that you can use the properties of the new label in setting the properties of the new TextBox.

```
Option Explicit

Private WithEvents txtNewBox As TextBox
Private Sub Form_Load()
Dim lblALabel As Label

  Me.WindowState = vbMaximized
  Me.Font.Size = 14

  Set lblALabel = Form1.Controls.Add("VB.Label", "AReallyNewLabel")
  Set txtNewBox = Form1.Controls.Add("VB.TextBox", _
                                      "AReallyNewTextBox")

  With lblALabel
    .Visible = True
    .Height = 300
    .Left = 0
    .Top = 0
    .AutoSize = True
    .Caption = "This is a new label that was added to identify " _
              & "the new text box!"
  End With
```

```
    With txtNewBox
      .Visible = True
      .Width = TextWidth("This new text box was not added at " _
                         & "design time! ")
      .Height = 300
      .Left = 0
      .Top = lblALabel.Height + 100
      .Text = "This new text box was not added at design time!"
    End With
    Me.Show
End Sub
Sub txtNewBox_GotFocus()
  MsgBox "You just entered the text box that was added at " _
          & "run time!"
End Sub
```

Obviously, you'll face many more issues when you add controls at runtime. First of all, event handling is much trickier when you're adding controls that are not already referenced via the Project ➔ Components dialog box in your project. In this case, you would have to declare the control with code such as the following,

```
Private WithEvents extCtl As VBControlExtender
```

and then use `Select Case` code in the `ObjectEvent` procedure, such as this:

```
Private Sub extObj_ObjectEvent(Info As EventInfo)
    Select Case Info.Name
    Case "Click"
       ' code for click event here.
     ' Other cases to handle
End Sub
```

Finally, if the component isn't referenced and it requires a license, then you'll need to add the license to the `Forms.Licenses` collection before you attempt to add the code.

CHAPTER 4

Disk and File
Tips and Tricks

THIS CHAPTER DEALS WITH DISKS AND FILES on a user's system. Visual Basic has never supported these two areas very well, so you often end up doing things the hard way. The new file system objects that I talk about at the end of this chapter do, however, simplify many disk and file manipulations. The downside of using these file system objects is that they increase the size of your application because you may need to include the required library. (The libraries are part of Windows 2000 but not necessarily part of earlier Microsoft operating systems.)

Getting a File Name from a Path
(Before Visual Basic 6)

Compatible with: All versions of Visual Basic
Applies to: File names

Oftentimes, you'll need to parse a file name from a path string for use in your code. Visual Basic 6 has made this a fairly simple task—just start at the end of the string and stop when you find the first backslash (see the next tip). Before Visual Basic 6, you had to loop through the string to accomplish this task (not the most efficient way of doing it). Then, you had to use the Right$ function to get the actual file name and you had to take into account the possibility that no "\" is to be found at all. That makes the code tricky:

```
Function GetFileNameI(FilePath As String) As String
Dim lCounter As Long
Dim sFileName As String
Dim bFound As Boolean
  For lCounter = Len(FilePath) To lCounter Step -1
    If lCounter = 0 Then
      Exit For
    End If
    If Mid(FilePath, lCounter, 1) = "\" Then
      sFileName = Right$(FilePath, Len(FilePath) - lCounter)
```

```
        bFound = True
        Exit For
    End If
  Next
  If Not bFound Then
    GetFileNameI = FilePath
    Else
      GetFileNameI = sFileName
  End If
End Function
```

Getting a File Name from a Path (After Visual Basic 6)

Compatible with: Visual Basic 6
Applies to: File names

With Visual Basic 6, you have at least three ways to get at the file name and all of them lead to cleaner code. The first is to simply use the new InstrRev function and work backward until you get to the last "\":

```
Function GetFileNameII(FilePath As String) As String
Dim lPos As Long
  lPos = InStrRev(FilePath, "\")
  GetFileNameII = Right$(FilePath, Len(FilePath) - lPos)
End Function
```

Notice that you don't have to worry about there not being a backslash—in this case you get the whole string because InstRev returns 0.

The next method uses the new Split function to get an array filled with the various parts of the full path.name.

Recall that the Split function takes any string and parses it into an array, based on a string delimiter. So now, you just need to use the Split function with a backslash as the delimiter. The last element of the array will be the file name.

Here is the same function from the previous listing implemented with the new Split function code.

```
Function GetFileNameIII(FilePath As String) As String
Dim aArray() As String
Dim sFileName As String
  aArray = Split(FilePath, "\")
```

```
  sFileName = aArray(UBound(aArray))
  GetFileNameIII = sFileName
End Function
```

The third method uses the new file system objects, which are discussed in the last tip in this chapter.

Creating a Full Directory Path

Compatible with: Visual Basic 32-Bit
Applies to: Directories

If you use built-in Visual Basic functions to create entire directory structures, you will need to do looping and constant error checking. There's an easier way to get the job done if you use API calls. The key is in the API functions found in the IMAGEHLP.DLL.

Declare

This is the Declare you need for the API function:

```
Public Declare Function MakeSureDirectoryPathExists Lib _
"IMAGEHLP.DLL" (ByVal DirPath As String) As Long
```

Code

The following code uses the MakeSureDirectoryPathExists function from the IMAGEHLP.DLL to create an entire directory with just one call.

```
Public Function CreatePath(NewPath) As Boolean
  'The function requires that there is a trailing "\"
  If Right$(NewPath, 1) <> "\" Then
    NewPath = NewPath & "\"
  End If
  If MakeSureDirectoryPathExists(NewPath) <> 0 Then
    'No errors so return True
    CreatePath = True
  End If
End Function
```

Example

Here is an example of how to use the CreatePath function. It returns False if some type of error occurred.

```
bReturn = CreatePath("c:\windows\drivers\mydrivers")
```

> **NOTE**   *The IMAGEHLP.DLL comes with Windows 95, Windows 98, and Windows NT.*

An Optional Way to Create a Full Directory Path

Compatible with: Visual Basic 32-Bit
Applies to: Directories

An alternative exists to using the IMAGEHLP.DLL to create a full directory path, just in case Microsoft decides to stop installing it in Windows someday. You can use the CreateDirectory API call instead.

Code

Use the following code as an alternative to using the IMAGEHLP.DLL.

```
Public Type SECURITY_ATTRIBUTES
  nLength As Long
  lpSecurityDescriptor As Long
  bInheritHandle As Long
End Type
Public Declare Function CreateDirectory Lib "kernel32" Alias _
          "CreateDirectoryA" (ByVal lpPathName As String, _
          lpSecurityAttributes As SECURITY_ATTRIBUTES) As Long
Public Function CreateNewDirectory(NewDirectory As String) _
                              As Boolean
Dim SecAttrib As SECURITY_ATTRIBUTES
Dim lReturn As Long
Dim lCounter As Long
Dim sTempDir As String
Dim aDirs() As String
  CreateNewDirectory = True
  On Error GoTo CreateNewDirectory_Error
  aDirs = Split(NewDirectory, "\")
```

```
  sTempDir = aDirs(0)
  For lCounter = 1 To UBound(aDirs)
    sTempDir = sTempDir & "\" & aDirs(lCounter)
    SecAttrib.lpSecurityDescriptor = &O0
    SecAttrib.bInheritHandle = False
    SecAttrib.nLength = Len(SecAttrib)
    lReturn = CreateDirectory(sTempDir, SecAttrib)
  Next
  Exit Function
CreateNewDirectory_Error:
  CreateNewDirectory = False
End Function
```

The CreateNewDirectory function will return False if any errors occurred.

Example

The following example shows you how to use the CreateNewDirectory function.

```
Dim bReturn as Boolean
  bReturn = CreateNewDirectory("c:\windows\drivers\mydrivers")
```

You can also use the file system objects shown at the end of this chapter to create directories.

Finding a File in Drives or Folders

Compatible with: Visual Basic 32-Bit
Applies to: Files

One common task most Visual Basic programmers need to accomplish is verifying the existence of a specific filename. More often than not, a simple call to the Dir$ function will suffice, *if* the path of the filename in question is known.

Sometimes, however, the path to that desired file is unknown, and doing a recursive search through all the sub and sub-sub folders that fill the directory structure of today's hard drives in an effort to locate the file is not terribly efficient.

The code that follows uses the SearchTreeForFile function from the IMAGEHLP.DLL. This function searches an entire drive for a file and returns back the path of where the file was found, including the file name. The one drawback to this function is that it will find only the first instance of the file. If you want to find multiple files with the same name, this function won't work for you.

Declare

To use the `SearchTreeForFile` function from the IMAGEHLP.DLL you'll need the following `Declare`.

```
Public Declare Function SearchTreeForFile Lib "IMAGEHLP.DLL" _
                        (ByVal lpRoothPath As String, _
                         ByVal lpInputName As String, _
                         ByVal lpOutputName As String) As Long
Public Const MAX_PATH = 260
```

Code

The following custom Visual Basic function can then find the specific file you're seeking.

```
Public Function FindFile(RootPath As String, _
                         FileName As String) As String
Dim lNullPos As Long
Dim lResult As Long
Dim sBuffer As String
  On Error GoTo FileFind_Error
  'Allocate buffer
  sBuffer = Space(MAX_PATH * 2)
  'Find the file
  lResult = SearchTreeForFile(RootPath, FileName, sBuffer)
  'Trim off Null if it's there
  If lResult Then
    lNullPos = InStr(sBuffer, vbNullChar)
    If Not lNullPos Then
      sBuffer = Left$(sBuffer, lNullPos - 1)
    End If
    FindFile = sBuffer
    Else
      FindFile = vbNullString
  End If
  Exit Function
FileFind_Error:
  'If there was an error, just return an empty string
  FindFile = vbNullString
End Function
```

Example

Here is an example of how to use the `FindFile` function.

```
sFileName = FindFile("C:\", "NWIND.MDB")
```

Assuming you have installed Visual Basic on the C: drive with the default locations, this will return

```
C:\Program Files\Microsoft Visual Studio\VB98\NWIND.MDB
```

as the value of `sFileName`.

Copying Files by Using Version Checking

Compatible with: Visual Basic 32-Bit
Applies to: Files

When copying program files such as DLLs or EXEs, you have to be careful not to copy over files that may be newer versions. Unfortunately, the Visual Basic FileCopy method blindly copies files with no version checking or even any date checking. The following code will safely copy a file to a new destination directory.

If version information is available for the file, this code will use that information to copy over files that are the same version or older. It copies over files that are the same version in case the file in the destination directory somehow got corrupted; this ensures that the "good" file will be copied over it. This code even goes the extra mile by checking the file dates if no version information is available.

Declare

The following code could and should be used to copy just about any file. Put the following code into a module file.

```
Private Type VS_FIXEDFILEINFO
   dwSignature As Long
   dwStrucVersionl As Integer     '  e.g. = &h0000 = 0
   dwStrucVersionh As Integer     '  e.g. = &h0042 = .42
   dwFileVersionMSl As Integer    '  e.g. = &h0003 = 3
   dwFileVersionMSh As Integer    '  e.g. = &h0075 = .75
   dwFileVersionLSl As Integer    '  e.g. = &h0000 = 0
   dwFileVersionLSh As Integer    '  e.g. = &h0031 = .31
```

```
                      dwProductVersionMSl As Integer ' e.g. = &h0003 = 3
                      dwProductVersionMSh As Integer ' e.g. = &h0010 = .1
                      dwProductVersionLSl As Integer ' e.g. = &h0000 = 0
                      dwProductVersionLSh As Integer ' e.g. = &h0031 = .31
                      dwFileFlagsMask As Long         ' = &h3F for version "0.42"
                      dwFileFlags As Long             ' e.g. VFF_DEBUG Or
                                                      '   VFF_PRERELEASE

                      dwFileOS As Long                ' e.g. VOS_DOS_WINDOWS16
                      dwFileType As Long              ' e.g. VFT_DRIVER
                      dwFileSubtype As Long           ' e.g. VFT2_DRV_KEYBOARD
                      dwFileDateMS As Long            ' e.g. 0
                      dwFileDateLS As Long            ' e.g. 0
                   End Type
                   Private Declare Function GetFileVersionInfo Lib "Version.dll" _
                      Alias "GetFileVersionInfoA" (ByVal lptstrFilename As String, _
                      ByVal dwhandle As Long, ByVal dwlen As Long, lpData As Any) _
                      As Long
                   Private Declare Function GetFileVersionInfoSize Lib "Version.dll" _
                      Alias "GetFileVersionInfoSizeA" _
                      (ByVal lptstrFilename As String, lpdwHandle As Long) As Long
                   Private Declare Function VerQueryValue Lib "Version.dll" Alias _
                      "VerQueryValueA" (pBlock As Any, ByVal lpSubBlock As String, _
                      lplpBuffer As Any, puLen As Long) As Long
                   Private Declare Sub MoveMemory Lib "kernel32" _
                      Alias "RtlMoveMemory" (dest As Any, ByVal Source As Long, _
                      ByVal length As Long)
```

Code

This function retrieves the version or date information for a file and copies the file
if necessary. If the file does not exist in the destination directory, this code copies
it over to that directory without performing any checks.

```
Public Function SafeFileCopy(sFileName As String, _
                             sOrigPath As String, _
                             sDestinationPath As String) _
                             As Boolean
Dim sSourceVer As String
Dim sDestinationVer As String
Dim bCopyFile As Boolean
  On Error GoTo FileCopy_Error
```

```
'Fix directory paths if needed
If Right(sDestinationPath, 1) <> "\" Then
  sDestinationPath = sDestinationPath & "\"
End If
If Right(sOrigPath, 1) <> "\" Then
  sOrigPath = sOrigPath & "\"
End If
'If File is not in the destination path, go ahead and copy it
If Len(Dir$(sDestinationPath & sFileName)) = 0 Then
  FileCopy sOrigPath & sFileName, sDestinationPath & sFileName
  bCopyFile = True
  Else
    'Get version
    sSourceVer = GetFileVersion(sOrigPath & sFileName)
    sDestinationVer = GetFileVersion(sDestinationPath & _
                                     sFileName)
    'If no version, check for date
    If Len(sSourceVer) = 0 And Len(sDestinationVer) = 0 Then
      If CDbl(FileDateTime(sOrigPath & sFileName)) >= _
          CDbl(FileDateTime(sDestinationPath & sFileName)) Then
          'Original file has a later date
          bCopyFile = True
      End If
      Else
        'We have version info
        If sSourceVer >= sDestinationVer Then
          bCopyFile = True
        End If
    End If
    'Do the file copy
    If bCopyFile Then
      Kill sDestinationPath & sFileName
      FileCopy sOrigPath & sFileName, sDestinationPath & _
               sFileName
    End If

  End If
  SafeFileCopy = bCopyFile
FileCopy_Error:
  'Do nothing, will return back False
End Function
```

Code

The following function uses Windows API calls to retrieve version information from a file. It will return the version information if it is available or an empty string if it isn't available.

```
Private Function GetFileVersion(FileName As String) As String
Dim lBufferLen As Long
Dim lDummy As Long
Dim aBuffer() As Byte
Dim lVerPointer As Long
Dim ffiVerBuffer As VS_FIXEDFILEINFO
Dim lVerBufferLen As Long
Dim lReturn As Long
Dim sFileVer As String
  lBufferLen = GetFileVersionInfoSize(FileName, lDummy)
  If lBufferLen < 1 Then
    'No File Info
    Exit Function
  End If
  'Get Version Info from API calls
  ReDim aBuffer(lBufferLen)
  lReturn = GetFileVersionInfo(FileName, 0&, lBufferLen, _
                               aBuffer(0))
  lReturn = VerQueryValue(aBuffer(0), "\", lVerPointer, _
                          lVerBufferLen)
  MoveMemory ffiVerBuffer, lVerPointer, Len(ffiVerBuffer)
  'Get the File Version
  sFileVer = Format$(ffiVerBuffer.dwFileVersionMSh) & "." & _
             Format$(ffiVerBuffer.dwFileVersionMSl) & "." & _
             Format$(ffiVerBuffer.dwFileVersionLSh) & "." & _
             Format$(ffiVerBuffer.dwFileVersionLSl)
  GetFileVersion = sFileVer
End Function
```

Example

The following sample code shows how to use the SafeFileCopy function. The function will return True if the file was copied, and False if it was not copied or if an error occurred.

```
Dim bReturn As Boolean
bReturn = SafeFileCopy("vote.gif", "c:\temp", _
                       "c:\website\images")
```

You can find this code in the modVerFileCopy.bas file in the Chapter 4 directory, which is among the source code available for download from the Apress Web site (see the Introduction for more information).

Copying Files with a Progress Indicator

Compatible with: Visual Basic 32-Bit
Applies to: Files

The biggest drawback to the Visual Basic FileCopy method is that it lacks a means of showing your users the progress of the file copying process (that is, how much of the copying is completed and how much is left to be done). The danger in this is if you are copying a large file, a user might think that your program has locked up.

Users have their own internal clocks that govern how long they will wait before they start wildly clicking buttons, menus and such on your program in an attempt to get it to do something. To avoid this, you must give users some way of knowing what your program is up to.

The easiest way to show the progress of the copy procedure is with a modal Form that provides users with text or a progress bar, such as the one that comes in the Microsoft Common Windows Controls OCX. Instead of using the Visual Basic FileCopy method, you need to open up the files and copy, chunk by chunk, the data from the original file to the destination file. This gives you time in between each chunk to update the status for the user.

I've wrapped up the code in a class file. (See the FileCopy.vbp project in the Chapter 4 directory that can be downloaded from the Apress Web site). This class has a method called FileCopy that does the chunk-by-chunk copying of the file, and raises events to give feedback to the code that uses it. The FileCopy method uses the Visual Basic Open, Get, and Put methods to do the actual file copying. To provide the feedback, you would raise the custom CopyStart, CopyEnd, and CopyProgress events in the class as appropriate.

Creating the clsFileCopy Class

Start off by creating a new class file and call it clsFileCopy. Next, put the following code in the Declaration section of the class.

```
Private lBuffSize As Long
Public Event CopyStart()
Public Event CopyEnd()
Public Event CopyProgress(PercentDone As Byte)
```

You are going to allow the developer who is using this class to pick the size of the chunks (buffer) it will copy over in each gulp. Remember: The smaller the buffer, the more feedback you can give the user, but the copy process will take longer. This obviously calls for a property that the user of the class can set. In this case, I'm using the Initialize event to give this property a default value of 25,000:

```
Public Property Get BufferSize() As Long
  BufferSize = lBuffSize
End Property
Public Property Let BufferSize(ByVal BuffSize As Long)
  lBuffSize = BuffSize
End Property
Private Sub Class_Initialize()
  'Setup Default
  lBuffSize = 25000
End Sub
```

FileCopy Function

The following code for the FileCopy function will do the file copying and return False if any errors occurred during the copy process.

```
Public Function FileCopy(SourceFileName As String, _
                         TargetFileName As String) As Boolean
Dim lCounter As Integer
Dim lSrcFileNum As Integer
Dim lTarFileNum As Integer
Dim lSrcFileSize As Long
Dim sBuffer As String
  'Setup default return value
  FileCopy = True
  On Error GoTo FileCopy_Error
  lSrcFileSize = FileLen(SourceFileName)
  'Setup Buffer
  sBuffer = Space$(BufferSize)
  'Delete the target file
  If Len(Dir$(TargetFileName)) Then
    Kill TargetFileName
  End If
  RaiseEvent CopyStart
  'Open the files
  lSrcFileNum = FreeFile
  Open SourceFileName For Binary Access Read As lSrcFileNum
```

```
    lTarFileNum = FreeFile
    Open TargetFileName For Binary Access Write As lTarFileNum
    'Copy File
    For lCounter = 1 To lSrcFileSize \ Len(sBuffer)
      Get #lSrcFileNum, , sBuffer
      Put #lTarFileNum, , sBuffer
      RaiseEvent CopyProgress(CByte(lCounter * Len(sBuffer) / _
                              lSrcFileSize * 100))
      DoEvents
    Next
    'Copy any remaining portion
    sBuffer = Space$(lSrcFileSize - Loc(lTarFileNum))
    If Len(sBuffer) Then
      Get #lSrcFileNum, , sBuffer
      Put #lTarFileNum, , sBuffer
    End If
    Close lSrcFileNum
    Close lTarFileNum
    RaiseEvent CopyProgress(100)
    RaiseEvent CopyEnd
Exit Function
FileCopy_Error:
    FileCopy = False
    Exit Function
End Function
```

Example

Here is the code for the sample project FileCopy.vbp, which you can find in the
Chapter 4 directory of the source code download from the Apress Web site. This
project uses the Microsoft Common Windows Controls ProgressBar control to
show the status of the copy process.

Just use WithEvents when declaring the clsFileCopy class and it's ready to go!

```
Dim WithEvents mobjFileCopy As clsFileCopy
Private Sub cmdCopy_Click()
Dim bReturn As Boolean
  Set mobjFileCopy = New clsFileCopy
  mobjFileCopy.BufferSize = 1000
  bReturn = mobjFileCopy.FileCopy(App.Path & "\Northwind.mdb", _
                                  App.Path & "\Northwind.bak")
  Set mobjFileCopy = Nothing
End Sub
```

```
Private Sub mobjFileCopy_CopyEnd()
  DoEvents
  ProgressBar1.Value = 0
End Sub
Private Sub mobjFileCopy_CopyProgress(PercentDone As Byte)
  ProgressBar1.Value = PercentDone
End Sub
Private Sub mobjFileCopy_CopyStart()
  ProgressBar1.Value = 0
End Sub
```

Finding the Path of a Loaded File

Compatible with: Visual Basic 32-Bit
Applies to: Files

To find out where a file that is loaded in your project (such as a DLL or OCX) is executing from, just use this simple function.

Declare

First, you need the Declares that will let you use the GetModuleHandle API and the GetModuleFileName functions from Kernel32.

```
Public Declare Function GetModuleHandle Lib "kernel32" _
                    Alias "GetModuleHandleA" _
                    (ByVal lpModuleName As String) As Long
Public Declare Function GetModuleFileName Lib "kernel32" _
                    Alias "GetModuleFileNameA" _
                    (ByVal hModule As Long, _
                    ByVal lpFileName As String, _
                    ByVal nSize As Long) As Long
Public Const MAX_PATH = 260
```

Code

The GetLoadedFilePath will return the location of the loaded file, or an empty string if the file is not loaded.

```
Function GetLoadedFilePath(FileName As String) As String
Dim lModHandle As Long
Dim sPath As String
```

```
Dim lReturn As Long
    lModHandle = GetModuleHandle(FileName)
    sPath = Space(MAX_PATH)
    lReturn = GetModuleFileName(lModHandle, sPath, Len(sPath))
    GetLoadedFilePath = Left$(sPath, lReturn)
End Function
```

Example

Here's an example of one way you can use this function.

```
SLocation = GetLoadedFilePath("vb6.exe")
```

This line of code will return the following in the default installation of Visual Basic:

```
C:\PROGRAM FILES\MICROSOFT VISUAL STUDIO\VB98\VB6.EXE
```

See the sample LoadedFile.vbp project in the Chapter 4 directory of the source code that you can download.

Finding the Total Space Available on a Drive

Compatible with: Visual Basic 32-Bit
Applies to: Drives

Two API calls enable you find out how much space is available on a user's hard drive. The first, `GetDiskSpaceFree`, unfortunately was coded to return a Long, therefore it is unreliable for drives larger than 2GB—pretty much all drives in use today!

Starting with Windows 95 OSR2, Microsoft added another API called `GetDiskFreeSpaceEx` that uses a "large" integer type made up of two Words (16-bit unsigned integers). To use this API, first create a type for the large integers:

```
Private Type LARGE_INTEGER
  lowWord As Long
  highWord As Long
End Type
```

Next, you need a function to convert this type into a displayable number. Luckily the Visual Basic Currency type can handle enormously large integers, as such:

```
Private Function CCurLargeInt(Lo As Long, Hi As Long) As Currency
'This function converts the LARGE_INTEGER data type to the
'Currency data type which gives us plenty of room
Dim curLo As Currency
Dim curHi As Currency
  If Lo < 0 Then
    curLo = 2 ^ 32 + Lo
    Else
      curLo = Lo
  End If
  If Hi < 0 Then
    curHi = 2 ^ 32 + Hi
    Else
      curHi = Hi
  End If
  CCurLargeInt = curLo + curHi * 2 ^ 32
End Function
```

Here's the Declare for GetDiskSpaceFreeEx.

```
Private Declare Function GetDiskFreeSpaceEx Lib "kernel32" Alias _
    "GetDiskFreeSpaceExA" (ByVal lpRootPathName As String, _
    lpFreeBytesAvailableToCaller As LARGE_INTEGER, _
    lpTotalNumberOfBytes As LARGE_INTEGER, _
    lpTotalNumberOfFreeBytes As LARGE_INTEGER) As Long
```

And, finally, here's some code that uses all of this to get information on the state of the user's disk drive, such as the real space that's available.

```
Private Sub Form_Click()
Dim lResult As Long
Dim liAvailable As LARGE_INTEGER
Dim liTotal As LARGE_INTEGER
Dim liFree As LARGE_INTEGER
Dim curAvailable As Currency
Dim curTotal As Currency
Dim curFree As Currency

  'Determine the Available Space, Total Size and Free Space _
  'of a drive using the non buggy GetFreeDiskSpaceEx
  lResult = GetDiskFreeSpaceEx("c:\", liAvailable, _
                              liTotal, liFree)
  curAvailable = CCurLargeInt(liAvailable.lowWord, _
```

```
                                liAvailable.highWord)
  curTotal = CCurLargeInt(liTotal.lowWord, liTotal.highWord)
  curFree = CCurLargeInt(liFree.lowWord, liFree.highWord)

  Print "Available Space:  " & FormatNumber(curAvailable, 0) _
        & " bytes (" _
        & FormatNumber(curAvailable / 1024 ^ 3) & " G) " _
        & vbCr & "Total Space:       " _
        & FormatNumber(curTotal, 0) & " bytes (" _
        & FormatNumber(curTotal / 1024 ^ 3) & " G) " & vbCr _
        & "Free Space:        " _
        & FormatNumber(curFree, 0) & " bytes (" _
        & Format(curFree / 1024 ^ 3) & " G) "
End Sub
```

The New File System Objects

Compatible with: Visual Basic 32-Bit
Applies to: Files/Disks

It's taken a long time to get object-oriented file handling added to Visual Basic, but now that it is here, much of the code that you have seen in this chapter can be replaced by the more familiar Object.Method notation. Of course, the downside to using the new file system objects is that they require an extra library (except on Windows 2000) and also increase the footprint of your application.

The next few tips in this chapter demonstrate how you can benefit from these powerful new file system objects. In practice, the names properties and methods are so mnemonic that the IntelliSense feature of Visual Basic makes these objects mostly self-documenting.

To use the file system objects:

1. Add a reference to the Microsoft Scripting Runtime library. This DLL (scrrun.dll) comes with Internet Explorer 5, Microsoft Visual InterDev, Microsoft Internet Information Server, and Windows 2000. Be sure to get the latest version of the library. You can download it from the Microsoft Windows Script Technologies Web page at `http://msdn. microsoft.com/scripting`.
2. Create a new file system object via code, such as:

```
Set FSO = New FileSystemObject
```

At this point, you simply bank on the properties and methods of the FSO object. The FSO object has a property (FSO.Drives) that returns a collection of Drive objects. A Folders collection with Folder objects and a Files and Subfolders collection inside a Folder object are also available.

Retrieving Drive Information using File System Objects

Compatible with: Visual Basic 32-Bit
Applies to: Drives

I created a project to demonstrate how to use the Scripting Engine to retrieve drive information. The project name is DriveInfo.vbp and can be found in the Chapter 4 directory of the downloadable code (see the Introduction). The project loads up a ListView control with information about all the drives on the system.

The Scripting Engine has a Drives collection you can loop through using For Each. The collection returns a Drive object for each drive from which you can retrieve information. As you'll see, you're supplied with the drive letter, disk size information, the amount of free space, the machine's serial number, the volume name, and more.

> **NOTE** *Properties related to the space on a drive may be unreliable on some operating systems because of the bug in* GetDiskSpaceFree *(explained earlier in "Finding the Total Space Available on a Drive").*

Code

The following method fills a ListView control (part of the Microsoft common controls) with information about the drives.

```
Sub LoadDriveInfo()
Dim fsoDrives As New Scripting.FileSystemObject
Dim fsoDrive As Scripting.Drive
Dim mscItem As MSComctlLib.ListItem
Dim sTemp As String
  On Error Resume Next 'don't have break on all errors set!
  For Each fsoDrive In fsoDrives.Drives
    Set mscItem = ListView1.ListItems.Add
    mscItem.Text = fsoDrive.DriveLetter
    Select Case fsoDrive.DriveType
      Case Is = CDRom
```

```
        sTemp = "CD-ROM"
      Case Is = Fixed
        sTemp = "Fixed"
      Case Is = RamDisk
        sTemp = "Ram Drive"
      Case Is = Remote
        sTemp = "Remote"
      Case Is = Removable
        sTemp = "Removable"
      Case Is = Unknown
        sTemp = "Unknown"
    End Select
    mscItem.SubItems(1) = sTemp
    If fsoDrive.IsReady Then
      mscItem.SubItems(2) = fsoDrive.TotalSize
      mscItem.SubItems(3) = fsoDrive.AvailableSpace
      mscItem.SubItems(4) = fsoDrive.FreeSpace
      mscItem.SubItems(5) = fsoDrive.SerialNumber
      mscItem.SubItems(6) = fsoDrive.ShareName
      mscItem.SubItems(7) = fsoDrive.VolumeName
    End If
  Next
  Set fsoDrives = Nothing
  Set fsoDrive = Nothing
  Set mscItem = Nothing
End Sub
```

Using the Scripting Engine to Work Recursively on the Directory Structure

Compatible with: Visual Basic 32-bit
Applies to: Files

Traditionally, you had to cache the results of using Dir$ in order to work through the directory tree because Dir$ did not support recursion directly. This resulted in your project being filled with code like this:

```
'get sub-directories in the current directory
ReDim sSubDirs(5) <> 'allocate 5 items
sTmp = Dir$(sRoot + "*.*", vbDirectory)
Do While Len(sTmp) > 0
  If Left$(sTmp, 1) <> "." Then    'don't get "." and ".." entries
```

```
      If (GetAttr(sRoot + sTmp) And vbDirectory) = vbDirectory Then
        'add the directory name to the array
        sSubDirs(nSubDir) = sTmp
        nSubDir = nSubDir + 1
        If nSubDir = UBound(sSubDirs) Then
          'need to allocate 5 more items
          ReDim Preserve sSubDirs(nSubDir + 5)
        End If
      End If
    End If
    sTmp = Dir$
  Loop
```

The file system object directly supports recursion, which means the framework for this process can be as simple as the following (of course, you'll need to replace the comment do what you want with this folder with code).

```
Sub WorkWithSubFolders(   )
  Dim MoreFolders As Folders
  Dim TempFolder As Folder
  ' do what you want with this folder
  Set MoreFolders = AFolder.SubFolders
  For Each TempFolder In MoreFolders
    WorkWithSubFolders
  Next
End Sub
```

The following example simply fills a list box with all the files on a C: drive that have a fixed extension.

```
Private mobjFileSys As FileSystemObject

Private Sub Form_Load()
Dim strExt As String
Dim folTempFolder As Folder
Dim strStart As String
  strStart = "C:\"
  Me.Show
  Me.MousePointer = vbHourglass
  Set mobjFileSys = New FileSystemObject
  Set folTempFolder = mobjFileSys.GetFolder(strStart)
```

```
    strExt = InputBox("What extension to search for--don't use " _
                      & "a '.', example: tmp")
    WorkWithSubFolders folTempFolder, strExt
    Me.MousePointer = vbNormal
End Sub


Sub WorkWithSubFolders(ByVal AFolder As Folder, _
                       ByVal TheExtension As String)
Dim folsTempFilders As Folders
Dim folTempFolder As Folder
Dim filTempFile As File
    Me.Refresh
    DoEvents
    For Each filTempFile In AFolder.Files
      If mobjFileSys.GetExtensionName(filTempFile.Path) = _
         TheExtension Then
        List1.AddItem filTempFile.Path
      End If
    Next
    Set folsTempFilders = AFolder.SubFolders
    For Each folTempFolder In folsTempFilders
      WorkWithSubFolders folTempFolder, TheExtension
    Next
End Sub
```

As simple as it is conceptually, this code has a couple of interesting aspects to it. First off, you can see how easy it is to get the extension of a file name with the GetExtensionName method of the FileSystemObject. Next, notice the call to DoEvents and the call to Refresh. It is always a good idea when carrying out a complicated recursion to allow the events to be processed and refresh the screen from time to time.

I encourage you to use the Object Browser or to look through the documentation of the FileSystemObject to see the other methods and properties. It's a really cool object.

CHAPTER 5

Tips and Tricks to Use with Forms

BECAUSE FORMS CONSTITUTE THE BUILDING BLOCKS for 99 percent (or more) of your Visual Basic projects, you may end up using the tips in this chapter in virtually all your projects. You'll find a few tips that are out of the ordinary, such as how to make a non-rectangular Form or how to display a Form within a Form, that can be useful in more-specialized situations.

Adding a Form to the Add Form Dialog Box

Compatible with: Visual Basic 32-bit
Applies to: Forms

The Project → Add Form dialog box displays a list of the Form templates that Visual Basic knows about. The default location of these templates is the Template\Forms directory located below the spot where Visual Basic itself is stored. You can change this default location by using the options under the Environment tab on the Options dialog box. In any case, any Form you store in this directory will appear as a template Form in the Add Form dialog box.

Making a Form Elastic

Compatible with: Visual Basic 32-bit
Applies to: Forms

An *elastic Form* automatically resizes the controls on it in order to keep the controls proportionally sized when the Form is enlarged or shrunk. You can, of course, buy an elastic container control from a vendor such as VideoSoft, but it is nevertheless useful to know how to roll your own code to create an elastic Form.

The trick to writing elastic code is to think of the controls as being sized as a proportion of the elastic Form's dimensions. For example, if a TextBox's width is always `Me.ScaleHeight / 2`, regardless of how the Form is enlarged or reduced, the TextBox will always be half the size of the useable area of the Form.

For the sake of simplicity, I'm assuming no line controls or any other similar controls that do not have both a Height and Width are involved. Given this assumption, the following example demonstrates how to write elastic code.

1. Set up a type for the width, height, left, and top proportions, and an array to hold these values for each control on the Form. For instance:

```
Private Type ControlProportions
   sngWidthProportions As Single
   sngHeightProportions As Single
   sngTopProportions As Single
   sngLeftProportions As Single
End Type
Private maProportionsArray() As ControlProportions
```

2. Next, write a little routine that you will call from the Form_Initialize to fill the array with the correct proportions for the desired dimensions.

```
Private Sub InitProportionsArray()
Dim lngCounter As Long
   'For things like timer controls
   On Error Resume Next
   ReDim maProportionsArray(0 To Me.Controls.Count - 1)
   For lngCounter = 0 To Me.Controls.Count - 1
     With maProportionsArray(lngCounter)
       .sngWidthProportions = Me.Controls(lngCounter).Width / _
                              Me.ScaleWidth
       .sngHeightProportions = Me.Controls(lngCounter).Height / _
                               Me.ScaleHeight
       .sngLeftProportions = Me.Controls(lngCounter).Left / _
                             Me.ScaleWidth
       .sngTopProportions = Me.Controls(lngCounter).Top / _
                            Me.ScaleHeight
     End With
   Next
End Sub
```

3. For modularity's sake, put the code that uses this information in a routine (called ResizeControls in this example). All this routine does is employ the Move method to move the controls to where they should be if the proportions are to be kept intact.

```
Private Sub ResizeControls()
Dim lngCounter As Long
  On Error Resume Next
  For lngCounter = 0 To Me.Controls.Count - 1
    With maProportionsArray(lngCounter)
      'Move the controls to where they should be
      'resizing them proportionally
      Me.Controls(lngCounter).Move .sngLeftProportions * _
                     Me.ScaleWidth, _
                     .sngTopProportions * Me.ScaleHeight, _
                     .sngWidthProportions * Me.ScaleWidth, _
                     .sngHeightProportions * Me.ScaleHeight
    End With
  Next
End Sub
```

4. Finally, the Initialize event calls the InitProportionsArray routine to fill the array.

```
Private Sub Form_Initialize()
  InitProportionsArray
End Sub
```

5. It's then trivial to use the Resize event to call the ResizeControls procedure:

```
Private Sub Form_Resize()
  ResizeControls
End Sub
```

> **NOTE** *If you add controls dynamically at run time, either via a control array or by using the* Add *method, you'll need to modify the previous code to take into account that a new control was added.*

If you save a Form with this code attached to it as a template (see the previous tip in this chapter), then you'll have a handy way to add elastic Forms to your projects.

Making a Form Stay on Top of All Other Windows

Compatible with: Visual Basic 32-bit
Applies to: Forms

If you need to display a Form in Windows that will always appear on top of any other open window, you can do that easily with the SetWindowPos API call. The FormStayOnTop routine, which you'll see shortly, establishes the specified window as the TopMost window no matter which window is active.

All you need to do is pass to the routine the handle of the window you want to make TopMost (or for which you wish to end the TopMost setting) and a True/False flag to indicate whether the Form whose handle you pass should be TopMost or not.

Declare

Here's the Declare for the SetWindowPos API call.

```
Declare Function SetWindowPos Lib "user32" (ByVal hwnd As Long, _
                              ByVal hWndInsertAfter As Long, _
                              ByVal x As Long, ByVal y As Long, _
                              ByVal cx As Long, ByVal cy As Long, _
                              ByVal wFlags As Long) As Long
Public Const Swp_Nosize = &H1
Public Const SWP_Nomove = &H2
Public Const Swp_NoActivate = &H10
Public Const Hwnd_TopMost = -1
Public Const Hwnd_NoTopMost = -2
Public Const Swp_ShowWindow = &H40
```

Code

In the actual code, you make one of the parameters of Form type. You could also simply pass the window's handle of the Form as the parameter.

```
Sub FormStayOnTop(FormToSet As Form, OnTop As Boolean)
Dim lHwnd As Long
Dim lFlags As Long
Dim lPosFlag As Long
  lHwnd = FormToSet.hwnd
  lFlags = SWP_Nomove Or Swp_Nosize Or Swp_ShowWindow Or Swp_NoActivate
  Select Case OnTop
```

```
    Case True
      lPosFlag = Hwnd_TopMost
    Case False
      lPosFlag = Hwnd_NoTopMost
  End Select
  SetWindowPos lHwnd, lPosFlag, 0, 0, 0, 0, lFlags
End Sub
```

Example

To set your Form on top, call the following code.

```
Private Sub Command1_Click()
  FormStayOnTop Me, True
End Sub
```

To change your Form back to its normal state, call this code.

```
Private Sub Command2_Click()
  FormStayOnTop Me, False
End Sub
```

Whenever your Form exits, call the following code to make sure that any call to set your Form to be on top is undone.

```
Private Sub Form_Unload(Cancel As Integer)
  FormStayOnTop Me, False
End Sub
```

Adding Items to a ControlBox Menu

Compatible with: Visual Basic 5 and 6
Applies to: Forms

You can't add a custom menu item to the ControlBox menu of the Forms in your programs by using intrinsic Visual Basic functions. What you need is a technique called *subclassing,* which is Windows-speak for intercepting some or all of the usual messages that are sent to windows, and then customizing them to suit your own purposes. (Technically speaking, subclassing is a term from object-oriented programming that refers to modifying an existing object while keeping some of its functionality.)

> **WARNING** *Subclassing is a potentially dangerous technique because it can easily crash Visual Basic and even Windows itself. Remember to save often and make backups of your code.*

To any subclassing code you must also add a key line of code, which will send the original Windows messages you will be intercepting back up the food chain. You'll see it in use in the code that follows, but the framework always looks like this:

```
CallWindowProc(lProcOld, hWnd, lMsg, wParam, lParam)
```

Forgetting to add this critical line of code will definitely make your system unstable and lead to a greater probability of crashing.

In addition, you must never end a program that uses callbacks with an End statement; you must unload the Callback function to restore Windows to its normal state using code such as this:

```
Private Sub Form_Unload(Cancel As Integer)
   'Set back control to original message handler, or you
   'will experience the mother of all crashes!
   SetWindowLong Me.hWnd, GWL_WNDPROC, lProcOld
End Sub
```

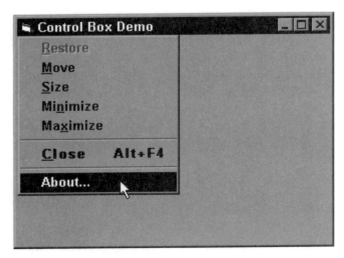

Figure 5-1. An About menu item added to a ControlBox

box, as my example code did, in your own project or write some custom code that does far more. It's that easy!

As I noted earlier: Do *not* terminate your program with an End statement or press the End button in the Visual Basic design environment. You must unload the callback with code such as this:

```
Private Sub Form_Unload(Cancel As Integer)
  'Set back control to original message handler, or you
  'will experience the mother of all crashes!
  SetWindowLong Me.hWnd, GWL_WNDPROC, lProcOld
End Sub
```

> **WARNING** *If you fail to unload the callback in the way I just stated, the Windows message pump will continue to pump messages to your application and very bad things can and* will *happen! It bears repeating: Do* not *use* End *in your project, or press the End button, or step through your code in the Visual Basic design mode. You have been forewarned!*

In short, subclassing and callbacks give you unprecedented power because you can change essentially anything that Visual Basic typically does. But, like any powerful techniques, you must use them correctly!

Tileing a Bitmap across a Form

Compatible with: Visual Basic 32-bit
Applies to: Forms

Have you ever wanted to spice up your Visual Basic forms (with an introductory splash screen, for instance) by tiling graphics such as you see on some Web pages or on the Windows desktop?

Guess what? You can! The following step-by-step example shows you how to tile any type of graphic the Visual Basic PictureBox can handle on a Form (see Figure 5-2 for an idea of how this might look). The bitmap image in this example tiles down the left side and across the top of the entire Form area. This example also serves as a good introduction to using the ever-popular BitBlt API call to manipulate graphics.

Although you can use intrinsic Visual Basic code (that is, the PaintPicture method) to tile a bitmap across a Form, the resulting code isn't as elegant or as powerful as code that employs the BitBlt API call.

Figure 5-2. Example of tileing a graphic on a Form

1. Add the following Declare function to a code module.

    ```
    Public Const SRCCOPY = &HCC0020
    Public Declare Function BitBlt Lib "gdi32" (ByVal hDestDC _
             As Long, ByVal x As Long, ByVal y As Long, _
                 ByVal nWidth As Long, ByVal nHeight As Long, _
                 ByVal hSrcDC As Long, ByVal xSrc As Long, _
                 ByVal ySrc As Long, ByVal dwRop As Long) As Long
    ```

2. Create a Form and name it frmTileGraphic.

3. Add a Picture control and name it picTile.

4. Insert your favorite bitmap graphic into the PictureBox by setting the Picture property accordingly.

5. Put the following code into the Declarations section of the frmTileGraphic Form.

    ```
    Private lMaxHeight As Long
    Private lMaxWidth As Long
    Private lPicHeight As Long
    Private lpicWidth As Long
    Private bComplete As Boolean
    Private bLeftSide As Boolean
    Private bAcrossTop As Boolean
    ```

6. Set the following properties of the `picTile` control and initialize the various Form level variables in the `Form_Load` event code that follows.

```
Private Sub Form_Load()
  With picTile
    .AutoSize = True
    lpicWidth = .ScaleWidth
    lPicHeight = .ScaleHeight
    .Visible = False
  End With
  'Set the toggle variables
  bComplete = False
  bAcrossTop = False
  bLeftSide = False
  'Used for color when testing the tiling down the left side
  With Me
    .Show vbModeless
    .Refresh
  End With
    Print "Click Form To Change Tile Style!"
End Sub
```

7. Put the following code in the `Form_Paint` event to do the actual tileing of the graphic using the `BitBlt` function.

```
Private Sub Form_Paint()
Dim lPicHwnd As Long
Dim lFrmHwnd As Long
Dim lCol As Long
Dim lRow As Long
Dim lReturn As Long
  'Initialize the variables
  lPicHwnd = picTile.hDC
  lFrmHwnd = Me.hDC
  If bComplete Then
    For lRow = 0 To lMaxHeight Step lPicHeight
      'Paint each column in a row before going to the next row.
      For lCol = 0 To lMaxWidth Step lpicWidth
        'Returns non-zero if successful
        lReturn = BitBlt(lFrmHwnd, lCol, lRow, lpicWidth, _
                         lPicHeight, lPicHwnd, 0, 0, SRCCOPY)
      Next
    Next
```

```
      ElseIf bLeftSide Then
        For lRow = 0 To lMaxHeight Step lPicHeight
          'Returns non-zero if successful
          lReturn = BitBlt(lFrmHwnd, lCol, lRow, _
                           lpicWidth, lPicHeight, _
                           lPicHwnd, 0, 0, SRCCOPY)
        Next
      ElseIf bAcrossTop Then
        For lCol = 0 To lMaxWidth Step lpicWidth
          'Returns non-zero if successful
          lReturn = BitBlt(lFrmHwnd, lCol, lRow, _
                           lpicWidth, lPicHeight, _
                           lPicHwnd, 0, 0, SRCCOPY)
        Next
    End If
End Sub
```

8. Set the maximum height and width of the area you will be painting whenever the Form is resized.

```
Private Sub Form_Resize()
  lMaxHeight = Height \ Screen.TwipsPerPixelY
  lMaxWidth = Width \ Screen.TwipsPerPixelX
End Sub
```

9. And, you'll want to clean up after yourself, so here's the Form_Unload code.

```
Private Sub Form_Unload(Cancel As Integer)
  'Unload the Form competely and free up memory
  ' Deactivates the Form
  Unload Me
  ' Free memory by removing the Form object from memory
  Set frmTileGraphic = Nothing
  ' empties all variables in memory and terminates application
  End
End Sub
```

10. Finally, here's the Form_Click event code that does all the work. This code changes the type of tiling being done every time you click the Form.

```
Private Sub Form_Click()
Static lState As Long
```

```
        'Toggle between the way the Form is painted
        If lState = 0 Then
          bComplete = True
          bAcrossTop = False
          bLeftSide = False

          ElseIf lState = 1 Then
            bComplete = False
            bAcrossTop = False
            bLeftSide = True

          ElseIf lState = 2 Then
            bComplete = False
            bAcrossTop = True
            bLeftSide = False

        End If

        'Increment the counter.  Reset when we reach 3.
        lState = lState + 1
        If lState = 3 Then lState = 0

        'By refreshing, the Form the Form_Paint event will be
        'activated.
        Me.Refresh

    End Sub
```

To test this code, just run the project and click the Form. Each time you do this, the program will cycle though one of the three different graphic tiling modes!

Displaying Forms within a Form

Compatible with: Visual Basic 32-bit
Applies to: Forms

Displaying child Forms within a Form without having a MDI Parent or child Form is actually quite simple to do if you employ the SetParent API call. You can use the following technique to show information from other Forms or even create a wizard-type Form.

Declare

Here's the Declare for SetParent.

```
Public Declare Function SetParent Lib "user32" (ByVal hWndChild _
            As Long, ByVal hWndNewParent As Long) As Long
```

Code

The trick is to then pass the windows handle of the Form you want to act as the parent container for the "child Form" to the SetParent API. After you do this, the child Form will remain constrained to appear only within the parent's Form—just as MDI child Forms do.

Simply place the code that calls the SetParent routine in the Form_Load event of any Form in your project that you want to look like a "child" form of another Form. This requires passing the window's handle of the parent Form as the second parameter for SetParent. For example,

```
SetParent Me.hWnd, Form1.hWnd
```

Of course, you should replace Form1 with the name of whichever Form you want to be the parent of the child Form.

> **NOTE** *When you use code such as this, be sure to unload the child Forms before unloading the Form that is acting as their parent!*

Bringing MDI Forms to the Top

Compatible with: All versions of Visual Basic
Applies to: MDI Child Forms

If you like to use MDI Forms, you may at times want to make sure only one copy of any child Form exists at any given time.

If you use the following method to display child Forms, then no matter what is done to the Form, this code will always pop the child Form to the top if it exists or create the Form if it doesn't. This means that every Form that uses this code can only exist once when the program is running.

The trick to this code lies in searching the Forms collection to see if a child Form you wondering about already exists. Although you can check the Form.Caption property for a match, putting a unique name in the Form.Tag property works best because it allows you to alter the caption property to reflect the state of the Form without interfering with the logic of the code in the ShowChildForm routine.

Code

This code implements a look-through for the various tags of the loaded forms in your MDI project.

```
Sub ShowChildForm(ChildForm As Form, FormTag As String)
Dim lCounter As Long
  For lCounter = 0 To Forms.Count - 1
    With Forms(lCounter)
      If .Tag = FormTag Then
        'Child Already exists.
        'Make visible
        .Visible = True
        .Enabled = True
        'Enable
        .Enabled = True
        'Restore
        If .WindowState = vbMinimized Then
           .WindowState = vbNormal
        End If
        'Bring to the top
        .ZOrder 0
        Exit Sub
      End If
    End With
  Next
  'If not present then Show Form
  ChildForm.Show vbModeless
End Sub
```

Example

Here's an example of how to use the code I just described.

```
Dim frmNewLogIn As Form
Set frmNewLogIn = frmLogIn
ShowChildForm frmNewLogIn, "LogIn"
```

Making MDI Child Forms Act Modally

Compatible with: All versions of Visual Basic
Applies to: MDI Child Form

Visual Basic does not allow you to show any child Forms in a MDI project as a modal Form, that is, the equivalent of using Show with the vbModal constant. If you want to provide this type of functionality in your project, you need to more or less "fake it" by disabling all the child Forms except for the one you want to act modally.

Code

The following code disables all child Forms, except the one you want to act as modal.

```
Public Sub SetMDIChildModal(ChildForm As Form)
Dim lCounter As Long
  'Loop through Forms collection
  Do While lCounter < Forms.Count
    'Find Child Forms Only
    If Not TypeOf Forms(lCounter) Is MDIForm Then
      If Forms(lCounter).MDIChild Then
        'Disable it if it's not the Form we want to
        ' fake modal
        If Forms(lCounter).Name <> ChildForm.Name Then
          Forms(lCounter).Enabled = False
          Else
            'Just in Case the Form passed in was disabled
            Forms(lCounter).Enabled = True
        End If
      End If
    End If
    lCounter = lCounter + 1
  Loop
End Sub
```

Example

To use this routine, all you need to do is pass the name of the child Form that you want to behave as if it were modal.

```
SetMDIChildModal Form1
```

Because all the other Forms in the project have been disabled, they need to be enabled when the "fake" modal child Form is unloaded or is made inactive by some other action. To enable the other child Forms, just reverse what you did in the previously listed code, like so:

```
Public Sub SetAllChildrenEnabled()
Dim lCounter As Long
  'Loop through Forms collection
  Do While lCounter < Forms.Count
    If Not TypeOf Forms(lCounter) Is MDIForm Then
      'Find Child Forms Only
      If Forms(lCounter).MDIChild Then
        Forms(lCounter).Enabled = True
      End If
    End If
    lCounter = lCounter + 1
  Loop
End Sub
```

Automating an Options Dialog Form

Compatible with: Visual Basic 32-bit
Applies to: Forms

Most applications feature some sort of Options Dialog Form in which users can select and save custom settings. But it can be enormously tedious to write the code to save all those values to the Registration Database, and then read them all back.

To use the code supplied here for each custom setting that you want to save, you'll need to define "section" and "key" strings. (See the Visual Basic Help menu for GetSetting or SaveSetting for examples of how to do this.) For each control that you use to maintain a setting, put the name of the key in the control's Tag property.

Next, put the default value of that key in the control itself at design time (during the Form_Load). To define the Section name for the registry key, I suggest putting all the controls that will be in that section in a common container control with the desired section string set in the container control's Tag property. This is actually very convenient because controls are grouped into frames and other logical containers.

When no container control is available, use any kind of invisible container that supports a Tag property, or use the Tag property of the dialog Form itself for controls that will not be inside a container.

Code

With the code that follows, you can totally automate saving and retrieving settings for the Options dialog box. Just drop this code into your Options Dialog Form and you will never have to make a code change!

```
Public Sub GetOptions()
Dim ctrlOption As Control
  For Each ctrlOption In Me.Controls
    With ctrlOption
      If .Enabled Then
        If Len(.Parent.Tag & .Tag) Then
          If TypeOf ctrlOption Is TextBox Then
            .Text = GetSetting(App.ProductName, .Parent.Tag, _
                               .Tag, .Text)
          ElseIf TypeOf ctrlOption Is CheckBox _
                 Or TypeOf ctrlOption Is HScrollBar _
                 Or TypeOf ctrlOption Is VScrollBar _
                 Then
            .Value = GetSetting(App.ProductName, .Parent.Tag, _
                                .Tag, .Value)
          End If
        End If
      End If
    End With
  Next
End Sub
Public Sub SaveOptions()
Dim ctrlOption As Control
  For Each ctrlOption In Me.Controls
    With ctrlOption
      If .Enabled Then
        If Len(.Parent.Tag & .Tag) Then
          If TypeOf ctrlOption Is TextBox Then
            SaveSetting App.ProductName, .Parent.Tag, .Tag, .Text
          ElseIf TypeOf ctrlOption Is CheckBox _
                 Or TypeOf ctrlOption Is HScrollBar _
                 Or TypeOf ctrlOption Is VScrollBar _
                 Then
            SaveSetting App.ProductName, .Parent.Tag, .Tag, _
                        .Value
          End If
        End If
```

```
        End If
      End With
    Next
End Sub
```

> **NOTE** *Call* GetOptions *before showing the Form to the user (call it from* Form_Load). *Call* SaveOptions *whenever you need to save settings (usually from* Form_Unload *or in a button click).*

Creating Non-Rectangular Forms

Compatible with: Visual Basic 32-bit
Applies to: Form

I'm ending this chapter with something really different! You may be surprised to know that it's possible to create a non-rectangular Form in Visual Basic (see Figure 5-3 for an example). A non-rectangular Form can be made in any shape that you can construct using Win32 region functions.

Declare

The following SetWindowRgn Win32 API call from within Visual Basic is quite simple to use, but the results are pretty amazing.

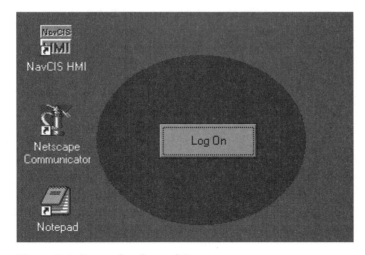

Figure 5-3. Example of a oval Form

```
Declare Function CreateEllipticRgn Lib "gdi32" (ByVal X1 As Long, _
                             ByVal Y1 As Long, ByVal X2 As Long, _
                             ByVal Y2 As Long) As Long
Declare Function SetWindowRgn Lib "user32" (ByVal hWnd As Long, _
                             ByVal hRgn As Long, _
                             ByVal bRedraw As Boolean) As Long
```

Example

By adding the following example code to the Form_Load that calls the previous two API functions, you can create a round Form as seen in Figure 5-3!

```
Dim lReturn As Long
  Me.Show
  lReturn = SetWindowRgn(Me.hWnd, CreateEllipticRgn(10, 25, 220, _
                                        200), True)
```

> **WARNING**   *Be sure that you do not close your program using the* End *function. If you do, Visual Basic will not unload the Form correctly.*

CHAPTER 6

Tips from the World of Windows API

AS YOU HAVE SEEN SO FAR IN THIS BOOK, as good as Visual Basic is, you often need to extend the capabilities of the programming language by using Windows APIs. Literally thousands of API calls are built into Windows, but many are safely wrapped in Visual Basic built-in functions so you don't need to worry about them. Nevertheless, a Visual Basic programmer can call just about any of them, so you can do practically anything a C++ programmer can do.

This chapter will explore some hard-to-find API calls and other API calls that add capabilities to the API wrappers beyond those that Visual Basic provides.

> **NOTE** *Although I show you how to accomplish many specific tasks with Windows API throughout this book, I obviously can't cover all the techniques you may find yourself using. There are two parts to learning to use the API: understanding how it works and knowing which functions to call. For the first part, the tutorial at the end of* Dan Appleman's Win32 API Puzzle Book and Tutorial for Visual Basic Programmers *from Apress is your best bet. His "Ten Commandments for Safe API Programming" in Appendix C of this book is taken from Appleman's* Win32 API *book. For the second part, the best reference to Windows API calls geared specifically to Visual Basic programmers is* Dan Appleman's Visual Basic Programmer's Guide to the Win32 API *(Sams).*

Detecting a Sound Card or Speaker Driver

Compatible with: Visual Basic 32-bit
Applies to: Sound

Here is a simple way to detect if a sound card (or speaker driver) is installed on a system. Add the following Declare to a Code module:

```
Declare Function waveOutGetNumDevs Lib "winmm.dll" () As Long
```

The previous function returns the number of wave output devices installed. If it returns 0, no devices exist, so you should use code like this because a non-zero number is interpreted as True:

```
If  waveOutGetNumDevs Then
  'sound card exists
Else
  'no sound card
End If
```

Launching Programs or Files from Your Application

Compatible with: Visual Basic 32-bit
Applies to: Applications

The Shell function in Visual Basic is limited in its functionality and ease of use. For example, you can use it when you have a .doc file and you want to launch Word to edit the file. To do this in general with Shell is tricky, though. You have to have the full path and executable name of the associated program *and* the original file's full pathname. If you don't supply this information, you will get the error shown in Figure 6-1.

Wouldn't it be easier to let Windows figure out which program opens up the file based on the settings in the Registration Database? And how about opening up a file from a Web site? The Visual Basic Shell function can't do that very easily either.

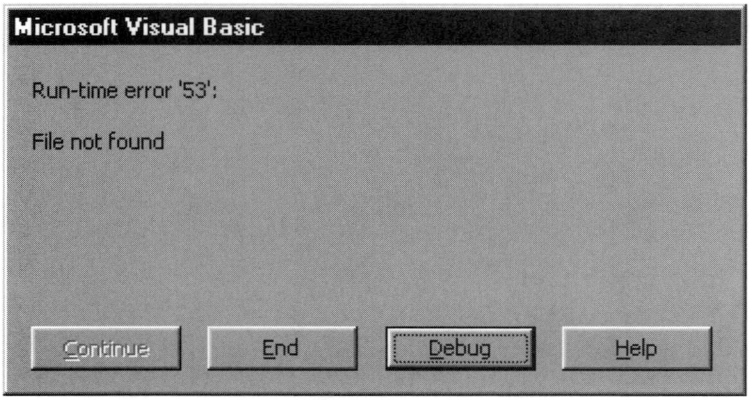

Figure 6-1. A Shell function error dialog box

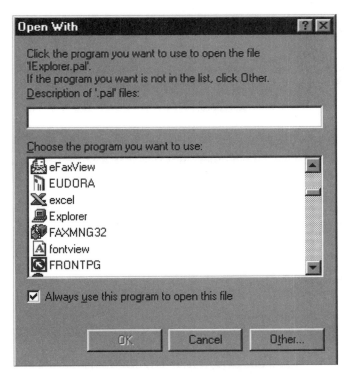

Figure 6-2. The Open With dialog box appears if a file does not have a program associated with it.

To gain much more functionality when launching a program or opening up a file with its associated program, use the Windows API ShellExecute call. The cool thing about the code in this tip is that if a file does not have a program associated with it, the Open With dialog box will appear (see Figure 6-2). This allows the user to pick which program will open the file. If the ShellExecute fails, the code generates an error message box letting the user know exactly what went wrong.

How to Use LaunchFile

In the code that follows, I have done all the hard work for you. All you need to do is call it. The parameters are as follows:

- **File** Full path together with the program or document name.

- **Verb** (optional)   With ShellExecute, you can either open the program or file or print it out. Use "Open" or "Print" to enable ShellExecute to do what you want. Leaving the verb blank will also open the program or file.

- **Parameters** (optional)   You can define command line parameters here for the program you are running.

- **ParenthWnd** (optional)   Here you set the hWnd handle of the Visual Basic Form or UserControl from which you are calling this subroutine.

Declare

The Declare follows. As with all API calls, you make this `Public` in a Code module.

```
Public Declare Function ShellExecute Lib "shell32.dll" _
                Alias "ShellExecuteA" (ByVal hwnd As Long, _
                ByVal lpOperation As String, _
                ByVal lpFile As String, _
                ByVal lpParameters As String, _
                ByVal lpDirectory As String, _
                ByVal nShowCmd As Long) As Long
```

Code

The `LaunchFile` subroutine follows. The `ShellExecute` API function requires the path and file to be kept separate. (You'll also use the `GetFileName` function found in Chapter 4 of this book.)

```
Public Sub LaunchFile(File As String, Optional Verb As String, _
                Optional Parameters As String, _
                Optional ParenthWnd As Long)
Dim sFile As String
Dim sPath As String
Dim lReturn As Long
Dim sMessage As String
  'Test incoming values
  If Len(Verb) = 0 Then
    Verb = "Open"
  End If
  If Len(Parameters) = 0 Then
    Parameters = vbNullString
  End If
  'Strip out the components of the file info we need
  sFile = GetFileName(File)
  sPath = Left$(File, Len(File) - Len(sFile))
  lReturn = ShellExecute(ParenthWnd, Verb, sFile, _
```

```
                    Parameters, sPath, vbNormalFocus)
'Check to make sure the shell went okay
Select Case lReturn
  Case Is = 31
    'There is no associated program for the specified file type
    'Give the user the choice on how to open the file
    sFile = "rundll32.exe shell32.dll,OpenAs_RunDLL " & sPath _
            & sFile
    lReturn = Shell(sFile, vbNormalFocus)
  Case 0
    sMessage = "System is out of memory, executable file is " _
              & "corrupt, or relocations are invalid."
  Case 2
    sMessage = "File was not found."
  Case 3
    sMessage = "Path was not found."
  Case 5
    sMessage = "Attempt was made to dynamically link to " _
              & "a task, or there was a sharing or " _
              & "network-protection error."
  Case 6
    sMessage = "Library required separate data segments " _
              & "for each task."
  Case 8
    sMessage = "There was insufficient memory to start the " _
              & "application."
  Case 10
    sMessage = "Windows version was incorrect."
  Case 11
    sMessage = "Executable file was invalid. Either it " _
              & "was not a Windows application or there " _
              & "was an error in the .EXE image."
  Case 12
    sMessage = "Application was designed for a different " _
              & "operating system."
  Case 13
    sMessage = "Application was designed for MS-DOS 4.0."
  Case 14
    sMessage = "Type of executable file was unknown."
  Case 15
    sMessage = "Attempt was made to load a real-mode " _
              & "application (developed for an earlier " _
              & "version of Windows)."
```

```
      Case 16
        sMessage = "Attempt was made to load a second instance " _
                    & "of an executable file containing " _
                    & "multiple data segments that were not " _
                    & "marked read-only."
      Case 19
        sMessage = "Attempt was made to load a compressed " _
                    & "executable file. The file must be " _
                    & "decompressed before it can be loaded."
      Case 20
        sMessage = "Dynamic-link library (DLL) file was invalid. " _
                    & "One of the DLLs required to run this " _
                    & "application was corrupt."
      Case 21
        sMessage = "Application requires Microsoft Windows 32-bit " _
                    & "extensions."
      Case Else
    End Select
    If Len(sMessage) > 0 Then
      'Display Error
      MsgBox sMessage, vbOKOnly + vbInformation, "Launch Error"
    End If
End Sub
```

For a quick reference, here's the version of the GetFileName function from Chapter 4 that uses Split.

```
Function GetFileName(FilePath As String) As String
Dim aArray() As String
Dim sFileName As String
  aArray = Split(FilePath, "\")
  sFileName = aArray(UBound(aArray))
  GetFileName = sFileName
End Function
```

Examples

The next few examples show you how to use the LaunchFile function. For instance, this example code launches Notepad:

```
LaunchFile "c:\windows\notepad.exe", , , Me.hwnd
```

You can also use `LaunchFile` to open files with the default program as config-ured in the Registration Database:

```
LaunchFile App.Path & "\vbtt.jpg", , , Me.hwnd
```

You can even open Web pages:

```
LaunchFile "http://www.vbtt.com", , , Me.hwnd
```

A sample project (FileLaunch.vbp) that corresponds to this tip can be found in the Chapter 6 directory in the code you can download from the Apress Web site (see the Introduction for more information).

Rolling Your Own GUIDs

Compatible with: Visual Basic 32-bit
Applies to: GUIDs

Do you need to create a unique identifier for your application? Why not use Global Unique Identifiers (GUIDs)? Microsoft claims GUIDs are guaranteed to be unique because they are based on

- The current date and time.

- A clock sequence and related persistent state to deal with the retrograde motion of clocks.

- A forcibly incremented counter to deal with high-frequency allocations.

- The globally unique IEEE machine identifier, obtained from a network card (the implementation does not require a network card; if a network card is not present, a machine identifier can be synthesized from highly variable machine states and stored persistently).

One company I worked for made frequent use of GUIDs to track items in a database. I have even used them to create unique temporary directories on disk drives for a Web server. Visual Basic 5 and 6 comes with a program that will create GUIDs for you, but the GUID program cannot be used in an application. Wouldn't it be nice to simply create GUIDs via code? Well, now you can by using the follow-ing sample code.

Declare

The first thing you need is a type for the GUID. Being a 16-byte unsigned number, it doesn't correspond to any built-in type in Visual Basic.

```
Private Type GUID
  Data1 As Long
  Data2 As Long
  Data3 As Long
  Data4(8) As Byte
End Type
```

Then, you need the Declare for the CoCreateGuid function.

```
Public Declare Function CoCreateGuid Lib "ole32.dll" _
    (pguid As GUID) As Long
Public Declare Function StringFromGUID2 Lib "ole32.dll" _
    (rguid As Any, ByVal lpstrClsId As Long, ByVal cbMax As Long) _
    As Long
```

Code

This function returns back a single GUID as a string (such as one you might see in the Registration Database).

```
Public Function GetGUID() As String
Dim udtGUID As GUID
Dim sGUID As String
Dim bytGUID() As Byte
Dim lRet As Long
Dim lLen As Long
  lLen = 40
  bytGUID = String(lLen, 0)
  CoCreateGuid udtGUID
  lRet = StringFromGUID2(udtGUID, VarPtr(bytGUID(0)), lLen)
  sGUID = bytGUID
  If (Asc(Mid$(sGUID, lRet, 1)) = 0) Then
    lRet = lRet - 1
  End If
  GetGUID = Left$(sGUID, lRet)
End Function
```

The interesting thing about this code is that it uses the VarPtr function, which is one of the hidden functions in Visual Basic. The VarPtr function returns the address of a pointer to the string data—a BSTR, which stands for Basic String because the format is different than "C" style strings. (See Dan Appleman's API tutorial book from Apress for more on BSTRs). Visual Basic has other hidden functions similar to VarPtr. They are called ObjPtr and StrPtr.

A sample project on the Apress Web site called guid.vbp in the Chapter 6 directory download for this book shows you how to use this code.

Verifying a User's Log-in Password

Compatible with: Visual Basic 32-bit
Applies to: Windows Operating System

By using an application I wrote for a past employer, my coworkers and I could send custom e-mail messages via Microsoft Exchange to approve document changes. But one drawback to Exchange and Outlook is that after you log in anyone can sit down at your computer and send e-mail messages under your name (not a very secure setup).

My coworkers and I wanted to verify that a user sending a message is logged into Windows 95/98 by making the user enter his or her user name and password when the custom e-mail (using a Visual Basic program as the message) was sent to Exchange Server.

I searched and searched on how to accomplish this, but had no luck. After posting a message on a newsgroup, I finally got the answer (which follows), and it's surprisingly easy! It's too bad that Microsoft made it so difficult for us to figure out.

Declare

Here's the Declare for the Wnetverify API that you need for the VerifyPassword function.

```
Public Declare Function WNetVerifyPassword Lib "mpr.dll" Alias _
    "WNetVerifyPasswordA" (ByVal lpszPassword As String, _
    ByRef pfMatch As Long) As Long
```

Code

Simply pass the password you want to check into the VerifyPassword function.

```
Public Function VerifyPassword(sPassword As String) As Boolean
Dim lReturn As Long
  If (WNetVerifyPassword(sPassword, lReturn)) <> 0 Then
    MsgBox "VerifyPassword: Application Error"
    Else
      If lReturn <> 0 Then
        VerifyPassword = True
      Else
        VerifyPassword = False
      End If
  End If
End If
End Function
```

> **NOTE** *The only drawback to the code in this tip is that it does not work on Windows NT. As soon as I find out how to verify a password on Windows NT, I will post the procedure on the VB Tips & Tricks Web site under the link for this book (see Appendix A of this book for more information on the Web site).*

Getting the Current User's Name

Compatible with: Visual Basic 32-bit
Applies to: Windows Operating System

This easy-to-use code provides the name of the user currently logged into Windows 95/98 or Windows NT. The name will be the one the user types into the Log In dialog box when the operating system starts.

Declare

Here's the Declare that you need to use in the GetMachineUserName function.

```
Public Declare Function WNetGetUser Lib "mpr.dll" Alias _
                  "WNetGetUserA" (ByVal lpName As String, _
                  ByVal lpUserName As String, _
                  lpnLength As Long) As Long
```

Code

The following function will return the user name as a string.

```
Public Function GetMachineUserName() As String
Dim sUserName As String
Dim lUserNameLen As Long
Dim lReturn As Long
  sUserName = Space(256)
  lUserNameLen = Len(sUserName)
  lReturn = WNetGetUser(ByVal Clng(0), sUserName, lUserNameLen)
  If lReturn = 0 Then
    'Success - strip off the null.
    GetMachineUserName = Left(sUserName, _
                            InStr(sUserName, Chr(0)) - 1)
      Else
        GetMachineUserName = vbNullString
  End If
End Function
```

Getting a Machine Name

Compatible with: Visual Basic 32-bit
Applies to: Windows Operating System

Here's really cool function that gets the name of the computer the user is logged onto in Windows 95/98 or Windows NT. This code provides the name of the computer as defined in the Network dialog box under the Control Panel.

Declare

You need to use the following Declare in the GetMachineName function.

```
Public Declare Function GetComputerName Lib "kernel32" _
          Alias "GetComputerNameA" (ByVal lpBuffer As String, _
          nSize As Long) As Long
```

Code

You can use the following function to return back the machine name as a string.

```
Public Function GetMachineName() As String
Dim lSize As Long
Dim sBuffer As String
  sBuffer = Space$(256)
  lSize = Len(sBuffer)
  If GetComputerName(sBuffer, lSize) Then
    GetMachineName = Left$(sBuffer, lSize)
  End If
End Function
```

Opening or Closing the CD-ROM Door

Compatible with: Visual Basic 32-bit
Applies to: The CD-ROM drive

If you ever need to open or close a CD-ROM door to slide the disc tray out of the drive, the following code gives you an easy way to do that.

Declare

Here's the Declare you need for the OpenCDDoor and CloseCDDoor function.

```
Public Declare Function mciSendString Lib "winmm.dll" _
       Alias "mciSendStringA" (ByVal lpstrCommand As String, _
       ByVal lpstrReturnString As String, ByVal uReturnLength _
       As Long, ByVal hwndCallback As Long) As Long
```

Code

Use the following subroutine to open the CD-ROM door.

```
Public Sub OpenCDDoor()
  mciSendString "Set CDAudio Door Open Wait", _
                CLng(0), CLng(0), CLng(0)
End Sub
Use the following subroutine to close the CD-ROM door.
Public Sub CloseCDDoor()
  mciSendString "Set CDAudio Door Closed Wait", _
                CLng(0), CLng(0), CLng(0)
End Sub
```

If you want to find out how to write a program that will enable a user to do various things with a CD-ROM, such as playing or changing tracks, check out the Media Control Interface (winmm.dll) in the Visual Studio help directory or the Visual Basic API viewer.

Getting a List Separator Based on Geographic Locale

Compatible with: Visual Basic 32-bit
Applies to: Windows 32-bit

When you display a series of values, it probably looks something like this:

100, 200, 300

The problem with this treatment is that in some countries the comma carries a completely different meaning. For instance, commas in Germany have the same meaning as decimal points in the United States. The following table shows some list separators used by programmers in various countries.

COUNTRY	LIST SEPARATOR
France	;
Germany	;
Mexico	,
Sweden	;
United States	,

Whenever you need to display a list of values, use the following code. You can find out what the user's list separator is based on the operating system's local settings.

Declare

These are the constants and Declare that you need to use.

```
'Constant for default locale on default computer
Public Const LOCALE_USER_DEFAULT = &H400
'Constant for list seperator
Public Const LOCALE_SLIST = &HC
```

```
Public Declare Function GetLocaleInfo Lib "kernel32" Alias _
                "GetLocaleInfoA" (ByVal Locale As Long, _
                ByVal LCType As Long, _
                ByVal lpLCData As String, _
                ByVal cchData As Long) As Long
```

Code

The function that follows returns back the appropriate list separator based on the user's locale.

```
Public Function ListSeparator() As String
Dim lReturn As Long
Dim sSeparator As String
  'Set the string buffer to maximum
  sSeparator = Space(256)
  'Get the list separator from the API call
  lReturn = GetLocaleInfo(LOCALE_USER_DEFAULT, LOCALE_SLIST, _
                          sSeparator, Len(sSeparator))
  'If the call was succesful
  If lReturn Then
    'Clear off the empty spaces and need to subtract 1 from
    'lReturn because it adds a null character
    sSeparator = Left$(sSeparator, lReturn - 1)
  End If
  ListSeparator = sSeparator
End Function
```

> **TIP**   *Be sure to check out the other information available through the* GetLocaleInfo *API call. You can retrieve all types of information about numbers, currency, time, and data formatting as configured in the Regional Settings Properties in the Windows Control Panel.*

Creating Improved DoEvents for NT Users

Compatible with: Visual Basic 32-bit
Applies to: Windows NT

The Visual Basic DoEvents function is a great way to keep a tight process from hogging the system. In Windows NT 4, however, you'll find your CPU usage reaching 100 percent very quickly.

Try adding a line with `Sleep 1` after `DoEvents` to your tight loops. The `Sleep` function will delay the application by only one millisecond, and if you call the sleep command every 150 or 200 passes, the delay is even shorter. When I tested this on my NT machine, calling `Sleep` after every 200 loops cut my CPU usage to about 92% of capacity. I dropped the parameter for the `Sleep` function to 10 and my usage was cut to 1%. Be aware that your mileage may vary depending on the type of machine this code is run on.

Declare

Here's the Declare that you need for the example code that follows.

```
Public Declare Sub Sleep Lib "Kernel32" (ByVal dwmilliseconds As Long)
```

Example

The following example shows you how to use the `Sleep` API call.

```
Private Sub Command1_Click()
Dim lCounter As Integer
  Do
    'Your Process code goes here
    For lCounter = 1 To 10000
      DoEvents
      If lCounter Mod 200 = 0 Then
        Sleep 1
      End If
    Next
  Loop
End Sub
```

Adding Pop-Up Help to Your Program

Compatible with: Visual Basic 32-bit
Applies to: Applications

Adding quick help capabilities to a program is getting easier these days with the popular tool tips seen in almost every major application. Although tool tips can provide some guidance to the user, any help information they give must be stated in only a few words.

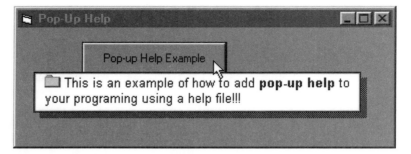

Figure 6-3. Example of pop-up help added to a program

What if you want to give your users a little more on-screen help without making them journey all the way into your application's help file? What if you also want to include a graphic? You can't do either with tool tips, but you can by linking directly to a help topic from a Windows help file (see Figure 6-3). It's much easier than you'd imagine.

Declare

You'll need the following Declare for the sample code coming up.

```
Public Const HELP_CONTEXTPOPUP = &H8&
Public Declare Function WinHelp Lib "user32" Alias "WinHelpA" _
            (ByVal hwnd As Long, ByVal lpHelpFile As String, _
            ByVal wCommand As Long, ByVal dwData As Long) _
            As Long
```

Example

This code will display a Help pop-up when the user right-clicks the button.

```
Private Sub Command1_MouseDown(Button As Integer, _
                                Shift As Integer, X As Single, _
                                Y As Single)
Dim lReturn As Long
  If Button = vbRightButton Then
    'The last parameter is the topic context ID number
    lReturn = WinHelp(Me.hwnd, App.Path & "\MYHELP.HLP", _
                    HELP_CONTEXTPOPUP, 1010)
  End If
End Sub
```

The pop-up help will stay on screen until the user presses any key or mouse button (just like with a Help file).

Adding Quick Search to ListBoxes and ComboBoxes

Compatible with: Visual Basic 32-bit
Applies to: ListBox/ComboBox

You can always just search through items one at a time if you have a box with thousands of entries, but that would be rather inefficient. The ubiquitous SendMessage windows API call is the trick here.

Declare

Here's the Declare for the SendMessage API call.

```
Declare Function SendMessage Lib "user32" Alias "SendMessageA" _
        (ByVal hwnd As Long, ByVal wMsg As Long, _
        ByVal wParam As Long, ByVal lParam As Any) As Long
```

You'll also need one of four constants depending on whether you want an exact match and whether you're dealing with a ListBox or ComboBox:

```
Public Const LB_FINDSTRING = &H18F
Public Const LB_FINDSTRINGEXACT = &H1A2
Public Const CB_FINDSTRING = &H14C
Public Const CB_FINDSTRINGEXACT = &H158
```

Example

Add a ListBox (lstBoxToSearch) and a TextBox (txtSearch) to a Form, and then add the following code to the Form_Load.

```
Private Sub Form_Load()
Dim lCounter As Long
  For lCounter = 1 To 20000
    If lCounter = 15000 Then
      lstBoxToSearch.AddItem "Find me!"
      Else
        lstBoxToSearch.AddItem Trim(Str(lCounter))
    End If
  Next
```

```
    lstBoxToSearch.AddItem "Wow!"
End Sub
```

Now, in the Change event for the TextBox, add the following.

```
Private Sub txtSearch_Change()
Dim sTempString As String
Dim lTheHandle As Long
Dim lPosition As Long
  sTempString = txtSearch.Text
  lTheHandle = lstBoxToSearch.hwnd
  If Len(sTempString) = 0 Then
   lstBoxToSearch.ListIndex = 0
    Else
    'Set the list index to the matching entry
    ' or first entry if nothing found
    lPosition = SendMessage(lTheHandle, _
      LB_FINDSTRING, -1, sTempString)
    If lPosition = -1 Then
      lstBoxToSearch.ListIndex = 0
      Else
        lstBoxToSearch.ListIndex = lPosition
    End If
  End If
End Sub
```

Because you are using the LB_FINDSTRING constant instead of the LB_FINDSTRINGEXACT constant, the moment you hit the "f" key, you immediately go to the 15,000 place in the ListBox!

CHAPTER 7

Tips on Visual Basic and the Internet

THIS CHAPTER OFFERS TIPS ON USING VISUAL BASIC with Internet applications, plus some tips for making Visual Basic work more effectively with IIS, the Microsoft Internet Information server.

Many of the tips in this chapter show you how to take advantage of the various components or libraries supplied with Internet Explorer. In a very real sense, Internet Explorer is nothing more than a couple of extraordinarily sophisticated ActiveX controls with some extra code thrown in for coordination purposes. This suggests that you can build a special-purpose browser with very little code or add one of the standard internet protocols, such as FTP, to your Visual Basic application very easily.

Using the WebBrowser Control to Build a Customized Browser

Compatible with: Visual Basic 32-bit
Applies to: WebBrowser

At the heart of Internet Explorer 4 and later versions is a DLL with the strange name SHDOCVW.DLL (which stands for *shell doc view*). This DLL handles common tasks such as displaying HTML, navigating to new URL, and so on. The DLL, in turn, is encapsulated into the WebBrowser ActiveX control, which you can add to your toolbox by selecting the Microsoft Internet Controls checkbox found under Project ➔ Components.

To see how easy it is to build a primitive application with browser capability, just follow these steps:

1. Start up a new project.

2. Add the Microsoft Internet Controls to the toolbox by selecting Project ➔ Components.

3. Add the WebBrowser control to a Form.

4. Add a TextBox named txtURL to the top of the Form.

5. Add the following code to the Form_Resize event.

```
Private Sub Form_Resize()
  txtURL.Move 0, 0, Me.ScaleWidth, Me.FontSize * 1.5
  WebBrowser1.Move 0, txtURL.Height + 30, Me.ScaleWidth, Me.ScaleHeight
End Sub
```

6. Now, to have the WebBrowser control actually display the page, you can use code like this:

```
Private Sub txtURL_KeyPress(KeyAscii As Integer)
  If KeyAscii = vbKeyReturn Then
    WebBrowser1.Navigate Trim(txtURL.Text)
  End If
End Sub
```

This browser admittedly is rather primitive and you will need quite a bit more code to have a fully functioning, special-purpose browser (including error trapping to deal with the common problem of some sites not being available). Nevertheless, you can easily imagine parsing the contents of the text box that gives the URL before calling the Navigate method. This allows you to restrict which URLs your special purpose browser is allowed to visit.

> **NOTE** *You can add an Internet Transfer Control to examine the* contents *of a page before displaying it in the Web Browser control (see "Using the Internet Transfer Control to Smart Mine the Web" later in this chapter). By doing this, you can prevent a young child, for instance, from seeing a page that contains certain phrases.*

The WebBrowser control properties and methods are available in the online Help. Because their names are for the most part mnemonic, they're quite easy to use.

Using the Application Wizard to Build Your Special-Purpose Browser

Compatible with: Visual Basic 32-bit
Applies to: Visual Basic Project

Figure 7-1. A MDI browser built with the Application Wizard

The Application Wizard supplied with Visual Basic is a mixed blessing, but it does work well for building the framework for Internet-enabled applications. In particular, the Application Wizard has the ability to build browsing capability into the applications it constructs and the ability to build MDI forms. Combine the two features and you have an easy way to create an MDI browser. (One of the more annoying features of Internet Explorer is that you have to open multiple versions of it to browse multiple sites.)

Figure 7-1 is an example of what you can get by using the Application Wizard without any tweaking (as yet) of the code it generated. Notice how multiple sites are shown in different MDI child windows.

The browsing form created by the Application Wizard contains the following:

- The Web browser control for displaying the HTML.

- A ComboBox for entering a new URL and keeping track of previously entered URLs. (The ComboBox is inside a PictureBox for reasons that escape me.)

- A Toolbar/Image List combination for buttons such as the one for a Home location.

- A Timer control used for figuring out when to display status messages.

The code generated by the Application Wizard is easy to understand, so adding new functionality to it is also simple. For example, as you might expect from its name, the `Download_Complete` event is triggered when the Web page is fully downloaded. The code generated by the Application Wizard is simply this:

```
Private Sub brwWebBrowser_DownloadComplete()
  On Error Resume Next
  Me.Caption = brwWebBrowser.LocationName
End Sub
```

This code places the URL in the caption of the child form when the download is complete. I recommend that you work through the code generated by the Application Wizard for an MDI-based, browser-enabled application. When you combine this with the online help, you'll have everything you need to build a full-featured, special-purpose browser.

Watching for Backslashes in Web Addresses

Compatible with: Visual Basic 32-bit
Applies to: WebBrowser

Windows uses the backslash character ("\") as its path separator, whereas many Web servers use the forward slash ("/") character for this purpose. The `Navigate` method in the WebBrowser control is smart enough to understand that if you wish to navigate to a local file that it should accept both the forward slash and backslash.

UNIX-based Web sites probably won't be able to do this conversion. For this reason, you should use the new `Replace` function on any URL passed to the `Navigate` method, as such:

```
txtURL.Text = Replace(txtURL.Text, "\","/")
```

Printing HTML Documents with the WebBrowser Control

Compatible with: Visual Basic 32-bit
Applies to: Printing HTML

The WebBrowser control has the added ability of printing HTML documents. At work, I use the Internet Explorer control to print hundreds of HTML documents at a time. You can even arrange it so that the user never needs to interact with the control.

To print the currently loaded HTML document, or a file or URL, you need to use the ExecWB method of the WebBrowser control. You can do a lot with the ExecWB method, but I'll just focus on printing here.

The following subroutine will print an HTML file. You merely need to send it your WebBrowser object and a file name (a URL address can be used, too).

```
Public Sub PrintHTML(HTMLControl As WebBrowser, FileName As String)
  HTMLControl.Navigate FileName

  Do Until HTMLControl.ReadyState = READYSTATE_COMPLETE
    Debug.Print "Waiting for control to load"
    DoEvents
  Loop
  HTMLControl.ExecWB OLECMDID_PRINT, OLECMDEXECOPT_DONTPROMPTUSER
End Sub
```

> **NOTE** *Make sure the control is done loading the document before trying to print.*

Next, the code goes into a DoEvents loop until the ReadyState property comes back as READYSTATE_COMPLETE. Then, you are ready to print by using ExecWB and a few parameter settings.

In the first parameter, you send the OLECMDID_PRINT constant to tell the control to print. In the second parameter, you send the OLECMDEXECOPT_DONTPROMPTUSER constant. This tells the control to *not* show the printer dialog box. If you want to show the printer dialog box to allow the user to change the target printer, for instance, you can change it to the OLECMDEXECOPT_PROMPTUSER constant.

I've used this code in a Visual Basic DLL with no problems. Because the WebBrowser control needs to be placed on a Form, I just use an invisible Form that the user never sees.

Using the Internet Transfer Control to Smart Mine the Web

Compatible with: Visual Basic 32-bit
Applies to: Internet Transfer Control

The (invisible) Microsoft Internet Transfer Control (msinet.ocx) allows you to get files from Web servers using the two standard protocols: HTTP (hypertext transfer protocol to get a page's raw HTML) and FTP (file transfer protocol). The following example demonstrates how you can use the Internet Transfer Control.

Suppose you don't want your special-purpose browser to display any pages with the words "Java Technology" on them. You need to get the raw HTML, parse it for the phrase "Java Technology," and then display the page only if the phrase *isn't* found. You can accomplish this using the simple browser that can be built using the steps listed under "Using the Web Browser Control to Build a Customized Browser" earlier in this chapter.

1. Add the Microsoft Internet Transfer Control to your toolbox and then add it to the Form.

2. Change the KeyPress event to

```
Private Sub txtURL_KeyPress(KeyAscii As Integer)
Dim sTemp As String
  If KeyAscii = vbKeyReturn Then
    sTemp = Inet1.OpenURL(Trim(txtURL.Text))
      If InStr(sTemp, "Java Technology") Then
        MsgBox "We don't show these kinds of pages"
      Else
          WebBrowser1.Navigate Trim(txtURL.Text)
      End If
    End If
End Sub
```

Now, try to visit java.sun.com and see what happens!

Using the Internet Transfer Control to Get Stock Prices (And Other Kinds of Data Mining)

Compatible with: Visual Basic 32-bit
Applies to: Internet Transfer Control

The principles of using the Microsoft Internet Transfer Control (msinet.ocx) to mine the Web are the same no matter which site you visit. You need to

• Send the request in a form the Web site can handle.

• Then, figure out how the data is hidden in the raw HTML.

For example, if you go to www.cnnfn.com and enter a stock symbol such as qqq (the Nasdaq 100 tracking stock), you'll see that the URL sent to the CNN Web server is

```
http://qs.cnnfn.com/tq/stockquote?symbols=qqq
```

If you look at the Web Page via View → Source in Internet Explorer, you get something like Figure 7-2.

As the highlighted line in Figure 7-2 shows, the stock price for QQQ may be found in the raw HTML line that looks like this:

```
<b><center>last:  221 5/8</center></b></font></td>
```

Now, all you have to do now is pass the following line to the OpenURL method of the Internet Transfer Control.

```
http://qs.cnnfn.com/tq/stockquote?symbols=qqq
```

Then, parse the resulting (large) string for the following:

```
<b><center>last:  221 5/8</center></b></font></td>
```

Note that you no longer need the WebBrowser control for this type of application.

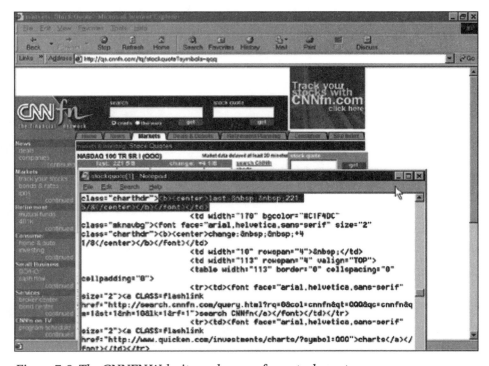

Figure 7-2. The CNNFN Web site and source for a stock quote page

The following example provides the sort of code you'll need, assuming that the TextBox (txtTicker) contains the ticker symbol and you farm out the parsing work to a routine called GetStockPrice. The following code also assumes you have named the TextBox as txtTicker but kept the default names for all the other controls (such as Inet1 for the Internet Transfer Control).

```
Private Sub txtTicker_KeyPress(KeyAscii As Integer)
Dim sTemp As String
  If KeyAscii = vbKeyReturn Then
    Me.MousePointer = vbHourglass
    MsgBox "The stock with ticker symbol " _
            & txtTicker.Text & " is " _
            & GetStockPrice(txtTicker.Text), _
            , "Stock Price"
  End If
  Me.MousePointer = vbNormal
End Sub


Function GetStockPrice(sTicker As String) As String
Dim sTemp1 As String
Dim sTemp2 As String
Dim lLoc As Long
  sTemp1 = Inet1.OpenURL("http://qs.cnnfn.com/tq/" _
                        & "stockquote?symbols=" _
                        & sTicker)
  lLoc = InStr(sTemp1, "<b><center>last:  ")
  lLoc = lLoc + Len("<b><center>last:  ")
  If lLoc = 0 Then
    GetStockPrice = "Ticker symbol not found!"
      Else
      Do Until Mid(sTemp1, lLoc, 1) = "<"
        sTemp2 = sTemp2 & Mid(sTemp1, lLoc, 1)
        lLoc = lLoc + 1
      Loop
    GetStockPrice = sTemp2
  End If
End Function
```

> **NOTE** *The kind of code I just listed relies on the format of the Web page not changing, otherwise the parsing code will no longer work. Therefore, this sort of code is best used when you have control of the raw HTML used on the Web site.*

Avoiding the OpenURL Method for Time-Consuming Data Transfers

Compatible with: Visual Basic 32-bit
Applies to: Internet Transfer Control

The OpenURL method of the Microsoft Internet Transfer Control (msinet.ocx) is certainly easy to use but it works *synchronously,* which can be a problem. The program waits until the transfer is complete before resuming, which means you have effectively put your program on hold whenever you use OpenURL. A better choice for time-consuming operations is to combine the Execute method with a call to DoEvents. The syntax of the Execute method is this:

```
object.Execute url, operation, data, requestHeaders
```

You can use both GET and POST for the operation value. (Check out any book on HTML for the distinction.)

The final step in using the Internet Transfer Control asynchronously is simply to put the correct code in the StateChanged event procedure. This event is triggered whenever any change occurs in the connection—for example, when data has arrived or is complete!

The State parameter in this event tells you what triggered the event. You then use the GetChuck method to retrieve the data from the Internet Transfer controls buffer. The header for the StateChanged event looks like this (assuming the default name of Inet1 for the Internet Transfer Control):

```
Inet1_StateChanged(ByVal State As Integer)
```

As far as getting data is concerned, the key state to check for is icResponseCompleted. The framework code will then look like this:

```
Private Sub Inet1_StateChanged (ByVal State As Integer)
'This framework assumes text is being downloaded
'not binary data
  Select Case State
  'place code for other states
  'NOTE: for really time consuming operations might want to check for
  'icResponseRecieved to conserve system resources
  'instead of waiting for completion via icResponse completed

  Case icResponseReceived
    Dim sTemp As String, sData As String
    Dim bDone As Boolean
```

```
            sTemp = Inet1.GetChunk(1024, icString)
         DoEvents 'to keep responsiveness up
         Do Until bDone
            sData = sData & sTemp
            DoEvents
            ' Get next chunk.
            sTemp = Inet1.GetChunk(1024, icString)
            If Len(sData) = 0 Then
               bDone = True
            End If
         Loop
      End Select
End Sub
```

Accessing IIS Objects from a Visual Basic ActiveX DLL

Compatible with: Visual Basic 6
Applies to: IIS Objects

In the mad rush to get custom Web sites up quickly, many companies have turned to Microsoft Internet Information Server (IIS) and Active Server Pages (ASP). Many of us who have used ASP technology have also discovered its shortcomings. ASP is a compile-on-demand interpreted language (much like the Visual Basic versions 1 through 4). It can be very slow, especially when using objects or doing looping in code. It uses only variant data types and debugging it in Visual Interdev is almost nonexistent; and the list goes on.

Many of us have turned to putting the majority of our code into Visual Basic ActiveX DLLs and calling them from ASP. This way, we get all the advantages of Visual Basic in the Web environment. Visual Basic projects are compiled to machine language now, so they are much faster than if they were done in ASP.

ASP pages have objects available to interact with the requests being sent to IIS. These objects are:

- **Application**: This object is used for sharing information among all users of a given application (Web site). This is most commonly used for database connection strings, directory locations, and such.

- **Request**: This object is used to retrieve information from or about the current user. It exposes all the information in the HTTP request. This is most commonly used object for retrieving information from a Form or values in the URL.

- **Response**: This object is used to return information to the user's browser. This is usually used for sending HTML back to the browser.

- **Server**: This object determines server-specific properties. This is also used to create your Visual Basic ActiveX DLLs in the same process space as the server.

- **Session**: This is similar to the Application object except that it stores information about the current Session (user) only. It can be used to keep information about the products the user might have put into his or her shopping cart.

> **NOTE**   *Be careful with what you store in the Session object. If you want to make sure your application scales well, do not store objects in this object. You should just stick to strings, numbers, and arrays.*

To use these objects from your DLL, you could pass these objects in the method call, but wouldn't it be simpler not to have to do that every time you make a call to your object? It so happens that you can access these IIS objects from within your DLL with just a few lines of code. First, you need to add the IIS objects to your Visual Basic project.

1. Go to the References dialog box and select the Microsoft Active Server Pages Object Library.

2. Then, place the following code in your Class file.

```
Private mobjIIS As ASPTypeLibrary.ScriptingContext
Public Function OnStartPage(myScriptingContext As ScriptingContext)
  Set mobjIIS = myScriptingContext
End Function
Public Function OnEndPage()
  Set mobjIIS = Nothing
End Function
```

The IIS server will call the OnStartPage function when your object is first created. This will set up the reference to the IIS objects. The IIS server will call the OnEndPage subroutine before it destroys your object so that the pointer can be released by setting it to Nothing. That's all there is to it! You can then use these objects the same way you would in ASP pages.

> **NOTE** *When calling your object from ASP, make sure you use* `Server.CreateObject`. *Otherwise, the reference to the IIS objects will not be made.*

You can find this code in the aspclass.cls in the Chapter 7 directory from the downloadable code on the Apress Web site (see the Introduction for more information).

I put this code in my \Microsoft Visual Studio\VB98\Template\Classes directory so that I can use it to create a new class that needs to access IIS. Because I've used this code, I no longer need to pass in the IIS object, but I usually pass in any information that the method might need.

Although I can get a lot of information from the Request object, such as Form variables, I choose to get just the information I need and pass it to the method. The reason for this is that if someone changes any field names, changing the ASP pages that might use a field name is much less work than recompiling a DLL and having to send it through the QA process.

The following example demonstrates how I've used this approach.

```
sDBConnect = Application("DBConnectString")
lMaxRsRows = Application("MaxRsRows")
lMaxResultRows = Application("MaxResultRows")
'Get values from the Form
sOrderID = Request.Form("orderid")
sFirstName = Request.Form("firstname")
sLastName = Request.Form("lastname")
lNameType = Request.Form("nametype")
lStartPos = Request.Form("startpos")
Set pfOperations = Server.CreateObject("pfOperations.Orders")
vData = pfOperations.SearchForOrders(sDBConnect, _
                                     sOrderID, sFirstName, _
                                     sLastName, lNameType, _
                                     lMaxRsRows, _
                                     lMaxResultRows, _
                                     lStartPos)
```

As you can see, I get the values I need from the Application and Request objects and pass them to the `SearchForOrders` function.

Determining whether RAS Is Connected

Compatible with: Visual Basic 32-bit
Applies to: Internet Connections

You can use this tip to determine if a computer is connected to the Internet via dialup networking, also known as Remote Access Service (RAS). However, this code will not detect if a computer is connected to the Internet via a LAN connection (including connections by cable modems).

Declare

You'll need to put the following code in a module file.

```
Public Const RAS95_MaxEntryName = 256
Public Const RAS_MaxDeviceType = 16
Public Const RAS95_MaxDeviceName = 128
Public Const RASCS_DONE = &H2000&
Public Type RASCONN95
  'set dwsize to 412
  dwSize As Long
  hRasConn As Long
  szEntryName(RAS95_MaxEntryName) As Byte
  szDeviceType(RAS_MaxDeviceType) As Byte
  szDeviceName(RAS95_MaxDeviceName) As Byte
End Type
Public Type RASCONNSTATUS95
  'set dwsize to 160
  dwSize As Long
  RasConnState As Long
  dwError As Long
  szDeviceType(RAS_MaxDeviceType) As Byte
  szDeviceName(RAS95_MaxDeviceName) As Byte
End Type
Public Declare Function RasEnumConnections Lib "RasApi32.dll" _
    Alias "RasEnumConnectionsA" (lprasconn As Any, _
    lpcb As Long, lpcConnections As Long) As Long
Public Declare Function RasGetConnectStatus Lib "RasApi32.dll" _
    Alias "RasGetConnectStatusA" (ByVal hRasConn As Long, _
    lpRASCONNSTATUS As Any) As Long
```

Code

This is the code for the IsRASConnected function. It will return True if a RAS connection exits.

```
Public Function IsRASConnected() As Boolean
Dim rasCon(255) As RASCONN95
Dim lG As Long
Dim lPCon As Long
Dim lReturn As Long
Dim rascStatus As RASCONNSTATUS95
  rasCon(0).dwSize = 412
  lG = 256 * rasCon(0).dwSize
  lReturn = RasEnumConnections(rasCon(0), lG, lPCon)
  If lReturn <> 0 Then
    MsgBox "ERROR"
    Exit Function
  End If
  rascStatus.dwSize = 160
  lReturn = RasGetConnectStatus(rasCon(0).hRasConn, _
                                rascStatus)
  If rascStatus.RasConnState = RASCS_DONE Then
    IsRASConnected = True
      Else
        IsRASConnected = False
  End If
End Function
```

You can find this code in the RasConnected.vbp sample project in the Chapter 7 directory on the downloadable code on the Apress Web site.

CHAPTER 8

Database Tips for Visual Basic and Microsoft Access

EVEN WITH THE GENERAL AVAILABILITY OF SQL SERVER, Microsoft Access is still not a bad choice for small- to medium-size databases. It just so happens that Visual Basic has a very good hook into Access databases.

You can use Access to generate Active Server Pages (ASPs), HTML, or traditional Access reports. And, because Access 2000 includes Visual Basic for Applications (VBA) 6.0, when you create Access reports, you can use VBA to control the report data, perform filtering, and more. The tips in this chapter can help you use Visual Basic to get even more out of Access.

The majority of the tips (unless otherwise noted) were written using the Microsoft Data Objects (DAO) version 3.6. You'll also find some tips on using the new 2.5 version of the Microsoft ActiveX Data Objects (ADO)!

Getting Up to Speed on Access Versions

The term *Jet* refers to an underlying (and unadorned) database engine that is used with most versions of Access. The latest version of Access can also use the new Microsoft Database Engine (MSDE), which is a trimmed-down version of SQL Server. Think of Access as a superset of Jet that includes the Access GUI, report builder, programming language, and so on. The Jet engine is also included with Visual Basic.

The following table lists information on the various versions of Access and the Jet engine. This table should help you see at a glance the relative power of the various versions of Access.

VERSION	RELEASE DATE	16/32 BIT	JET ENGINE VERSION
Access 1.0	12/92	16-bit	Jet 1.0
Access 1.1	5/93	16-bit	Jet 1.1
Access 2.0	4/94	16-bit	Jet 2.0
Access 2.0 SP1	10/94	16-bit	Jet 2.5
Access 95	11/95	32-bit	Jet 3.0
Access 97 Version7.0	1/97	32-bit	Jet 3.5
Access 2000	Q199	32-bit	Jet 4.0 (plus new Microsoft Database Engine, MSDE)
Pocket Access	Q199	32-bit (Win CE 2.1)	Jet 4.1

Three Secret Techniques to Document Your Code in Microsoft Access

As you probably already know, you should make it a practice to add comments, notes, and explanations to your code so that you and others can easily understand the purpose or logic to the code when it is read later on. In addition to allowing you to use the ever-popular apostrophe ('), one other little-known feature of Access is that it allows the use of Rem statements, line numbers, and line labels to document code in events and modules.

Rem Statement

Here's an example of a Rem statement.

```
MsgBox "This is another example": Rem <-- Comment goes here, after colon
```

Line Numbers

Line numbers can also be used to help document your code. A few rules to remember: They must be in the far-left column of your code, they must start with a digit (0–9), and they must be unique.

```
1    Dim lCounter As Integer
10     For lCounter = 1 To 10
20       Debug.Print "Hello World"
30     Next
```

Line Labels

Another documentation technique you have probably already seen in action is the use of line labels. In fact, the Microsoft Access Wizards use line labels in practically *every* code block they generate. Like line numbers, line labels must also start in the far-left column of your code, but they must begin with a character (A–Z) and end with a colon (:).

```
Private Function Y2KFix()
  If Date > #1/1/00# Then
    GoTo Cleanup 'Jump to Cleanup
    Else
      Rem Your code goes here.
  End If
Cleanup: 'Line Label
  Rem Bye-Bye
End Function
```

With all these features, plus the good old apostrophe, you have no excuses for failing to document your code!

Unloading Your Database Workspace

Compatible with: Visual Basic 32-bit
Applies to: Microsoft Access Database

Even though Visual Basic documentation states that when a method goes out of scope Visual Basic will clean up all the variables that were in use . . . don't believe it. I have found (and continue to find) that this is not always the case. Most of us have become used to setting objects to Nothing. Well, this step is even more important when you're working with databases. If something goes wrong, your database could stay locked and connections may not be released.

Code

To prevent your database from locking up, call the following method in your Form_Unload event or in your program's exit method.

```
Public Sub UnloadWorkspace()
Dim wsTemp As Workspace
```

```
Dim dbTemp As Database
Dim rsTemp As Recordset
  On Error Resume Next
  For Each wsTemp In Workspaces
    For Each dbTemp In wsTemp.Databases
      For Each rsTemp In dbTemp.Recordsets
        rsTemp.Close
        Set rsTemp = Nothing
      Next
      dbTemp.Close
      Set dbTemp = Nothing
    Next
    wsTemp.Close
    Set wsTemp = Nothing
  Next
End Sub
```

Dealing with Enter Keystrokes When Exporting Databases to Text Files

Compatible with: Visual Basic 6
Applies to: Microsoft Access Database

When programming in Visual Basic for a database application, you need to watch that you don't accept the Enter key. It can wreak havoc when you're exporting databases to text files. A problem doesn't exist with the database per se because the string in Visual Basic simply stores an Enter keystroke as Chr$(13) & Chr$(10) (also known as the vbCrLf constant). This value gets passed between the database and the application effortlessly.

The problem arises when you inevitably want to export the tables into a flat file. The text exports just fine except that the Chr$(13) & Chr$(10) values are converted back, effectively becoming Enter keystrokes once again, causing your export file to get out of whack. Then, when you want to import the file into the new (or old) tables, you get import errors galore and the import process stops.

The following work-around is very effective. First, you need to convert all the Chr$(13) & Chr$(10) values into something that DOS won't treat any differently than a regular character. It's unwise to use a keyboard character as your token because someone may type in that character when entering data into the database. Therefore, I recommend using Chr$(6)—an unprintable character.

Example

The following example demonstrates how to use this function.

```
rsData("Comments") = ReplaceEnter(txtComments.Text)
```

Code

The following is the code for this function.

```
Function ReplaceEnter(Text As String) As String
  ReplaceEnter = Replace(Text, vbCrLf, Chr$(6))
End Function
```

When the converted field that is filled with Chr$(6) needs to be displayed to the user, just reverse the process and convert the Chr$(6) values into Chr$(13) & Chr$(10).

Example

The following example demonstrates how to use this code.

```
txtComments.Text = ReplaceChr6(rsData("Comments") & vbNullString)
```

Code

Here's the code for removing the extra Chr$(6) values.

```
Function ReplaceChr6(Text As String) As String
  ReplaceChr6 = Replace(Text, Chr$(6), vbCrLf)
End Function
```

Avoiding SQL Query Problems from Erroneous Single Quotes

Compatible with: Visual Basic 6
Applies to: MS Access Database

With database applications, you may at times need to build SQL statements to Insert or Select based on what a user has entered into a TextBox. Given a simple example of a Select based on a user entering a last name of Jones, you might build a SQL statement to look like this:

```
sSQL = "Select * from Client where LastName = '" & txtLastName.Text & "'"
Set rsData = dbMyDatatbase.CreateSnapShot(sSQL)
```

Because LastName is defined as Text in the database, the value for the LastName field must be enclosed in single quotes. The SQL statement will then translate into:

```
Select * from Client where LastName = 'Jones'
```

This query will work fine. But, a problem arises when the user types a name such as O'Brien, for instance. The same SQL statement now looks like this:

```
Select * from Client where LastName = 'O'Brien'
```

Microsoft Access will return an error message saying that a syntax error exists in the query expression. How do you get around this? You can include single quotes in a query expression by turning that lone single quote into two single quotes.

Example

Here's an example of how to use this code.

```
sLastName = ParseQuotes(txtLastName.Text)
```

Code

The following code will do the parsing and convert the single quote.

```
Function ParseQuotes(Text As String) As String
  ParseQuotes = Replace(Text, "'", "''")
End Function
```

Now, the same Select (using sLastName as the replacement variable) will produce the following.

```
Select * from Client where LastName = 'O''Brien'
```

This version works great! By the way, you enter *two single quotes,* not one double quote. All of this becomes an issue for single quotes only. Double quotes are perfectly acceptable in a query expression.

Dealing with Null Database Fields

Compatible with: All Versions of Visual Basic
Applies to: Microsoft Access Database

By default, Access string fields contain NULL values unless a string value (including a blank string such as "") has been assigned. When you read these fields using Recordset into Visual Basic string variables, you get a runtime type-mismatch error.

> **NOTE**   *SQL Server 6.5 and earlier versions will automatically convert an Access NULL string field into a single-space string. Although this unfortunate behavior has been fixed in SQL Server 7.0 and later versions, it can yield unexpected results in certain situations.*

Example

The best way to avoid the problem of type-mismatch errors is to use the built-in & operator to concatenate a blank string to each field as you read it. You should also concatenate 0 for numeric fields.

```
Dim dbBiblio As Database
Dim rsData As Recordset
Dim sYear As String
Dim sHireDate As Date
Dim lReports As Long
  Set dbBiblio = OpenDatabase("Northwind.mdb")
  Set rsData = dbBiblio.OpenRecordset("Employees")
  'Concatenate empty string ("") here with null values
  sYear = rsData![Title] & vbNullString
  'Concatenate zero so it does not error
  sHireDate = rsData![HireDate] & 0
  lReports = rsData![ReportsTo] & 0
```

Filling a ComboBox with Data Quickly and Easily

Compatible with: All Versions of Visual Basic
Applies to: Microsoft Access Database

Filling in data from an Access database table doesn't have to be a huge chore. All the following method needs is an open database object, the name of the table, the field name to use, and, of course, the ComboBox object to fill with data. Be sure to set the Sorted property of the ComboBox to True.

Code

You can use the following example code to fill a ComboBox.

```
Public Sub FillComboBox(DBData As Database, TableName As String, _
                        FieldName As String, _
                        ComboToFill As ComboBox)
Dim rsData As Recordset
  'Clear the ComboBox
  ComboToFill.Clear
  'Set the Recordset
  Set rsData = DBData.OpenRecordset(TableName, dbOpenSnapshot)
  'Check whether there are any records
  If rsData.BOF Then
    Exit Sub
    Else
      Do While Not rsData.EOF
        'Check that the field is not a Null value else there will
         'be an error
        If rsData.Fields(FieldName) <> "" Or _
          Not IsNull(rsData.Fields(FieldName)) Then
            ComboToFill.AddItem rsData.Fields(FieldName)
        End If
        rsData.MoveNext
      Loop
      If ComboToFill.ListCount > 0 Then
        'Just to ensure that some item is selected
        ComboToFill.ListIndex = 0
      End If
  End If
  Set rsData = Nothing
End Sub
```

Example

Here's an example of how to use this code to fill a ComboBox with information from the `mdbData` database.

```
FillComboBox mdbData, "Products", "ProductName", Combo1
```

Of course, you have to open your database before calling this method, as such:

```
Set mdbData = OpenDatabase("Northwind.mdb")
```

> **NOTE** *The process I describe in this section can easily be used to also fill ListBoxes.*

Adding Security to Access Database Diagrams

You can prevent users from viewing any database diagrams in a user database by denying EXECUTE permissions on the `dt_getobjwithprop` and `dt_getpropertiesbyid` stored procedures. But, no way exists to selectively allow users access to some database diagrams and deny users access to others.

To secure database diagrams in a Microsoft Access project, try using these steps.

1. Open the sample Access project NorthwindCS.adp that is supplied with every copy of Access.

2. Select Tools ➔ Security ➔ Database Security.

To complete the next steps, you must use a logon and user account with System Administrator privileges when connecting NorthwindsCS.adp to its back-end data source.

3. On the Server Logins tab, click Add.

4. On the General tab, specify testUser in the Name text box.

5. Click the Database Access tab and grant testUser permission to access the NorthwindCS database.

6. Click OK.

7. In the SQL Server Security dialog box, click the Database Users tab.

8. Select testUser, click Edit, and then click Permissions.

9. Examine the list of objects in the database and locate the dt_getobjwithprop and dt_getpropertiesbyid stored procedures.

10. In the object list, DENY permission to EXECUTE those stored procedures.

11. Click Apply and then click OK to close the Database User Properties dialog box.

12. Close the SQL Server Security dialog box. In the Database window click Database Diagrams.

13. Double-click the database diagram named Relationships.

    Because you're currently connected to the SQL Server or MSDE as a system administrator, it should open.

14. Examine and close the database diagram.

15. Select File → Connection.

16. Modify the connection properties of your Access project so that you log on as testUser with no password.

17. Click Test Connection and then click OK to return to the Database window.

Note that the Relationships database diagram is no longer visible in the database diagram list.

Opening a Secured Access (Jet) Database with ADO

Compatible with: Visual Basic 32-bit
Applies to: Microsoft Access Database

You can open a secured Jet database using the ADO MSDataShape provider by using the following code.

```
cnn.Provider = "MSDataShape"
cnn.Open "Data Provider=Microsoft.Jet.OLEDB.4.0;" _
         & "Data Source=c:\nwind.mdb;User Id=Admin;" _
         & "Password=password;" _
         & "Jet OLEDB:System Database=c:\sysdb.mdw"
```

Or, you can use the code that follows to open the database.

```
cnn.Open "Provider=MSDataShape;" _
         & "Data Provider=Microsoft.Jet.OLEDB.4.0;" _
         & "Data Source=c:\nwind.mdb;User Id=Admin;" _
         & "Password=password;" _
         & "Jet OLEDB:System Database=c:\sysdb.mdw"
```

To open a database secured with a database password, use the following code.

```
cnn.Open "Provider=MSDataShape;" _
         & "Data Provider=Microsoft.Jet.OLEDB.4.0;" _
         & "Data Source=c:\nwind.mdb;" _
         & "Jet OLEDB:Database Password=DBPassword"
```

To open a database secured with both a database password and a user password, use the code that follows.

```
cnn.Open "Provider=MSDataShape;" _
         & "Data Provider=Microsoft.Jet.OLEDB.4.0;" _
         & "Data Source=c:\nwind.mdb;User Id=Admin;" _
         & "Password=password;" _
         & "Jet OLEDB:System Database=c:\sysdb.mdw;" _
         & "Jet OLEDB:Database Password=DBPassword"
```

For more information on migrating DAO to ADO, head to www.microsoft.com/data/ado/adotechinfo/dao2ado.htm.

Determining Which Version of the Microsoft Data Access Component You're Running

Applies to: Microsoft Data Access Component

The following table lists the various versions of the Microsoft Data Access Component (MSDAC) DLL. These DLLs supply the Microsoft data access components that are in common use.

MDAC VERSION	MSDADC.DLL	OLEDB32.DLL
MDAC 1.5c	1.50.3506.0	N/A
MDAC 2.0	2.00.3002.4	2.0.1706.0
MDAC 2.0 SP1	2.00.3002.23	2.0.1706.0
MDAC 2.0 SP2	2.00.3002.23	2.0.1706.0
MDAC 2.1.0.3513.2 (SQL 7 / 6.5 SP5a)	2.10.3513.0	2.10.3513.0
MDAC 2.1.1.3711.6 (IE5)	2.10.3711.2	2.10.3711.2
MDAC 2.1.1.3711.11 (GA)	2.10.3711.2	2.10.3711.9
MDAC 2.1 SP2	2.10.4202.0	2.10.4204.0
MDAC 2.5	2.50.4403.0	2.50.4403.8

Using the New Commands that Bring Access Closer to ANSI SQL

Applies to: Microsoft Access

Access has never been completely ANSI SQL compliant, but it's getting there. The following commands were altered or added in Access 2000/Jet 4.0 and are available via ADO 2.1 or higher.

ALTER TABLE	ADD USER
CREATE TABLE	ALTER DATABASE
CREATE PROCEDURE	ALTER USER
CREATE VIEW	CREATE GROUP
DROP PROCEDURE	CREATE USER
DROP VIEW	DROP GROUP
EXECUTE	DROP USER
BEGIN TRANSACTION	GRANT
COMMIT [TRANSACTION]	REVOKE
ROLLBACK [TRANSACTION]	

Working with ActiveX Data Objects

Compatible with: Visual Basic 32-bit

ADO (ActiveX Data Objects) is Microsoft's most current data model, and one that exposes the functionality of the OLE DB API. The three core components of the ADO model are the Connection, Command, and Recordset objects.

While the Connection object's function is fairly obvious and the Command object allows you to issue commands (typically SQL) directly to your data source, the Recordset object is the ADO workhorse. Its primary purpose is to send queries to the data source and return the results to the client application. You can supply the query via the Recordset Source property or programmatically.

Using the New Stream Object to Simplify File Handling

Compatible with: Visual Basic 32-bit

Beginning with ADO 2.5, which supports XML, you can also use the Stream object, as shown in the following example, to make file handling easier.

```
Dim stm as New ADODB.Stream
stm.Open "http://myserver01.mufolder/mydoc.txt"
stm.SaveToFile "c:\my documents\copyofmydoc.txt"
```

Returning a Disconnected Recordset Using ADO

Compatible with: Visual Basic 32-bit

As you'd probably guess, a disconnected Recordset is an ADO Recordset that no longer has a connection to the source database. In the following RetrieveCustomer function code, you can see how ADO sets the cursor location and opens a Recordset from the familiar Northwind database. (The Open method uses a previously defined DSN that points to a copy of your Access Northwind database.) The function returns a Recordset.

```
Option Explicit
Dim rs As ADODB.Recordset
Public Function RetrieveCustomers() As ADODB.Recordset
Dim sSQL As String
  Set rs = CreateObject("ADODB.Recordset")
  sSQL = "SELECT * FROM customers"
  rs.CursorLocation = adUseClient
  rs.Open sSQL, "Northwind", adOpenForwardOnly, adLockReadOnly
  Set RetrieveCustomers = rs
Exit Function
```

Example

Here's a simple example of how you can use the Recordset in a Visual Basic form.

```
Option Explicit
Dim oCustomer As ClientServices.Customer
Dim rsCustomer As ADOR.Recordset
Private Sub cmdGetCustomers_Click()
Dim sData As String
  Set oCustomer = New ClientServices.Customer
  Set rsCustomer = oCustomer.RetrieveCustomers()
  Do While Not rsCustomer.EOF
    sData = sData & rsCustomer("CompanyName") & vbCrLf
    rsCustomer.MoveNext
  Loop
  txtCustomers = sData
  Set rsCustomer = Nothing
End Sub
```

Returning Field Data from a Recordset

Compatible with: Visual Basic 32-bit
Applies to: Microsoft Access Database

It can become really annoying to have to write special-purpose code every time you need to extract field data from a Recordset. The following function will return field data from any Recordset that you pass it.

```
Function GetDataFromField(strTableName As String, strFieldName As String,
strCriteria As String) As Variant
Dim rstFieldData As New ADODB.Recordset
Dim strSQL As String
  On Error Resume Next
  strSQL = "SELECT " & strFieldName & " FROM " & strTableName _
      & " WHERE " & strCriteria
  rstFieldData.Open strSQL, DATA_CONNECTSTRING & DATA_PATH
  If Err = 0 Then
    GetDataFromField = rstFieldData(strFieldName)
    Else
      GetDataFromField = ""
  End If
End Function
```

Investing in Microsoft Office Developer

Don't confuse Microsoft Office 2000 Developer (MOD) with the Microsoft Office 2000 Resource Kit! Office 2000 Developer (its predecessor was called ODE for Office Developer Edition) is a VBA toolkit for Office developers, while the Resource Kit is a free set of utilities (www.microsoft.com/office/ork/2000/ appndx/toolbox.htm) aimed mainly at administrators.

Because MOD includes a full copy of Office 2000 Premium Edition (Word 2000, Excel 2000, PowerPoint 2000, Access 2000, Outlook 2000, Publisher 2000, FrontPage 2000, PhotoDraw 2000, and Small Business Tools) along with all the MOD tools and sample code, it's one of the best deals in town despite its price (as of this writing, $999 for MOD new users versus $799 for Office 2000 Premium new users).

The Code Librarian—a 2.7MB Access application—alone is worth the investment. It has *thousands* of code snippets and functions, all categorized for easy retrieval. Here's an example:

```
'For each project, build string to list each component's type
' and property values.
For Each vbpProj In vbeVBE.VBProjects
  ' Add this component's name and type to string.
  For Each vbcComp In vbpProj.VBComponents
    strMsg = strMsg & vbcComp.Name & " ("
    Select Case vbcComp.Type
      Case vbext_ct_StdModule
        strMsg = strMsg & "Standard Module)"
      Case vbext_ct_ClassModule
        strMsg = strMsg & "Class Module)"
      Case vbext_ct_MSForm
        strMsg = strMsg & "UserForm)"
      Case vbext_ct_Document
        strMsg = strMsg & "Document)"
      Case Else
        Stop
    End Select
    strMsg = strMsg & vbCr
    'List each of the component's properties and
    ' their values.
    For Each vbprProp In vbcComp.Properties
      strMsg = strMsg & vbTab & vbprProp.Name _
                 & vbTab & vbprProp.Value & vbCr
    Next vbprProp
  Next vbcComp
```

```
        'Call form to display component information for this project.
        With frmMsg
          .Caption = vbpProj.Name & " Component Information"
          .Controls("txtMsg").Value = strMsg
          .Controls("txtMsg").SetFocus
          .Controls("txtMsg").SelStart = 0
          .Show
        End With
        strMsg = ""
      Next vbpProj
    End Sub
```

Like its predecessors, Microsoft Office 2000 Developer includes the Access runtime, which lets you distribute Access applications royalty-free to customers and end-users who don't own Access. MOD also includes MSDE and licensing for royalty-free redistribution of the new Microsoft Data Engine, a 100-percent code-compatible desktop version of SQL Server 7.0.

Office VBA developers can also use the same Data Environment Designer (DED) and Data Report Designer that have been part of Visual Basic for some time. DED lets developers create, modify, and reuse hierarchical record set objects such as tables, views, SQL queries, and stored procedures as ActiveX Data Objects (ADO) components. The data report designer is a relatively lean "homegrown" report designer that's distinct from Seagate Software's Crystal Reports that has been part of Visual Basic for years.

Getting a Handle on Data Source Names

Compatible with: Visual Basic 32-bit

By using a DSN connection to a database, you can specify (through tools or code) a previously named data source to which you want your program connected. You (or a DBA) can create and name this source, which ends up as an ASCII text file. You use the Control Panel's ODBC applet to set up data sources.

What's the difference between System, User, and File DSNs? File DSNs keep their connection information in a file you can store anywhere, while System and User DSNs reside on the machines you create them on. As you might expect, a User DSN is associated with a single user, while a System DSN is associated with a system and can be used by several different users who may share the system.

Both User and System DSNs are faster than File DSNs. Of course, all DSN connections have an advantage over DSN-less connections in that you don't have to recompile if you have to change the database location.

Here is some code that will connect to a previously defined DSN via DAO (Data Access Objects).

```
Public Sub DAO_DSN_Connection()
Dim ws As Workspace
Dim db As Database
Dim rs As Recordset
Dim td As TableDef
  On Error GoTo DAO_DSN_ConnectionErr
  Set ws = Workspaces(0)
  Set db = ws.OpenDatabase("Northwind", dbDriverComplete, _
                           False, DSN=Northwind")
  Set rs = db.OpenRecordset("SELECT * from customers ", _
                           dbOpenSnapshot)
  'List the names of the tables in the TableDef collection
  For Each td In db.TableDefs
    If UCase$(Mid$(td.Name, InStr(td.Name, ".."), 4)) <> _
              ".SYS" Then
      strMsg = strMsg & "Table Name (" & td.Name & ")" & vbCrLf
    End If
  Next
  rs.Close
  db.Close
  ws.Close
  MsgBox strMsg, vbExclamation, APP_NAME
  Exit Sub
DAO_DSN_ConnectionErr:
  If errRoutine(Err, Error$(Err), _
                "frmMain:DAO_DSN_Connection") Then
    Resume
    Else
      Resume Next
  End If
End Sub
```

Becoming Familiar with Access 2000 Data Access Pages

A data access page (DAP) is a Web page that you can use to add, edit, view, or manipulate current data in a Microsoft Access or SQL Server database. You can create pages that are used to enter and edit data, similar to Access forms, and you can also create pages that display records grouped hierarchically, similar to Access reports.

To see what makes a data access page work, open it in Design view. You can examine the page layout and see the settings for the properties that make the page work. And, remember that you can store HTML code in fields in your database and display it as formatted HTML text on the page. For example, if a value in a field includes the HTML tag that formats text as italic (`<I>Text<I>`), you can use a bound HTML control on the page to display the value in italic text.

Enabling Row-Level Locking

Access 2000, just like SQL Server 7.0 and most RDBMSs, has row-level locking, a feature that's easy to overlook.

You enable the locking level with the new database option, Open databases using record level locking, which you can find by selecting Tools → Options and then clicking the Advanced tab. The actual level that is used depends on how the Access database is programmed.

Creating Crosstab Queries

Applies to: Microsoft Access Database

Jet uses the TRANSFORM and PIVOT keywords to make creating crosstabs fairly easy in Access, but bear in mind that if you want to create crosstabs in other data base management systems, such as SQL Server or Oracle, you have to write complex SQL SELECT statements (typically with INNER JOINs).

No matter which data source you employ, you'll probably want to use a ComboBox control to display the data so that users can substitute variables, such as ranges of dates.

Emulating Access Forms in Visual Basic

Compatible with: Visual Basic 32-bit
Applies to: Microsoft Access Database

Access master/child forms offer loads of advantages when you're working with data. If you want to emulate Access master/child forms in Visual Basic, use the Visual Basic hierarchical Recordset.

Giving the Right Password

Compatible with: Visual Basic 32-bit
Applies to: Microsoft Access Database

The default login/password for Access databases (.mdb extension) is Admin with no password. The default login/password for SQL Server is sa with no password. The default login/password for Oracle databases is scott/tiger (reputedly named after a developer and his cat).

Finding Important New Information on Integrating Access and SQL Server

A consolidated and annotated list of articles, tips, and resources related to integrating Access and SQL Server is available on the Web. You can find this vital new information at http://msdn.microsoft.com/isapi/msdnlib.idc?theURL=/library/techart/acsqlres.htm

Discovering Resources for Migrating from Access to SQL Server

A good place to start searching is with the free Access 97 upsizing wizard on the Microsoft Website at www.microsoft.com/AccessDev/ProdInfo/AUT97dat.htm. The wizard upsizes from Access 97 to SQL Server 6.5 or 7.0. The Access 2000 Upsizing tool that ships as part of Office 2000 supports only migration to SQL Server 7.0.

You may also want to refer to the Microsoft Knowledge Base Article Q237980 titled "How to Convert and Access Database to SQL Server," which can be found at http://support.microsoft.com/support. In addition, some third-party products are available at www.weirperf.com and www.ssw.com.au.

By the way, Apress will be publishing a book by Russell Sinclair (ISBN: 1-893115-24-0) on this important topic. It's called, naturally enough, *Moving from Access to SQL Server*. The book is scheduled to be published in Fall 2000.

Tips and Tricks on Some Advanced Stuff

THIS CHAPTER IS GEARED TO THOSE programmers who need to push Visual Basic that extra mile. To benefit from most of the tips listed here, you will need to be an experienced user of Windows API calls. You'll also find some tips on which files to install to get your Visual Basic program to run correctly, plus other helpful tidbits.

An Introduction to the AddressOf Operator

Compatible with: Visual Basic 5 and 6
Applies to: Message Callbacks

Unlike Microsoft Windows, the Visual Basic development environment is not based on a message-driven programming model. In Microsoft Windows, messages control most of everything that happens.

Visual Basic, on the other hand, supports a predefined set of events for each object (a Form or Control) that you create. This means that an application written in Visual Basic cannot respond to messages from Microsoft Windows that are not handled directly by a Visual Basic event. This might change some day, if we keep our fingers crossed, but for now you have to work around it.

For example, if you want to provide some help to a user whenever the user moves his mouse over menu items in your project, it can't be done with just Visual Basic functions. But with the use of Windows API calls and the Visual Basic AddressOf function, you can listen to all the messages that are being sent to your Form. When you find the appropriate message, you can then invoke some sort of action.

In the sample project for this tip, you will be looking for the WM_MENUSELECT message and displaying some help in the status bar. (See Figure 9-1 for an example of such a display.) You can find the example code in the addressof.vbp project in the Chapter 9 directory in the download for this title on the Apress Web site (see the Introduction for more information).

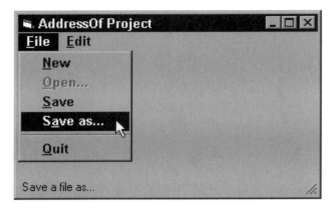

Figure 9-1. Using the AddressOf *function to display context-sensitive help*

The AddressOf function works like this: All Visual Basic methods live in memory when your project is running. Therefore, all methods have an address in memory that they are occupying. The AddressOf function returns that address to you for use in the SetWindowsHookEx API function. This function "hooks" into the Windows message queue so that you can intercept the messages coming to the Form.

Now take a look at how the AddressOf function is used in the sample project. First, you need to declare the following code in a module.

```
Private Type POINTAPI
  x As Long
  y As Long
End Type
Private Type MSG
  hWnd As Long
  Message As Long
  wParam As Long
  lParam As Long
  time As Long
  pt As POINTAPI
End Type
Private Const WH_MSGFILTER = (-1)
Private Const WM_MENUSELECT = &H11F
Private Const MSGF_MENU = 2
Private Const MF_BYCOMMAND = &H0&
Private Const MF_BYPOSITION = &H400&
Private Const MF_DISABLED = &H2&
Private Const MF_POPUP = &H10&
```

```
Private Declare Function SetWindowsHookEx Lib "user32" Alias _
                    "SetWindowsHookExA" (ByVal idHook As Long, _
                    ByVal lpfn As Long, ByVal hmod As Long, _
                    ByVal dwThreadId As Long) As Long
Private Declare Function UnhookWindowsHookEx Lib "user32" _
                    (ByVal mlhHook As Long) As Long
Private Declare Function CallNextHookEx Lib "user32" _
                    (ByVal mlhHook As Long, ByVal nCode As Long, _
                    ByVal wParam As Long, lParam As Any) As Long
Private Declare Function GetWindowThreadProcessId Lib "user32" _
                    (ByVal hWnd As Long, lpdwProcessId As Long) _
                    As Long
Private Declare Function GetMenuString Lib "user32" Alias _
                    "GetMenuStringA" (ByVal hMenu As Long, _
                    ByVal wIDItem As Long, _
                    ByVal lpString As String, _
                    ByVal nMaxCount As Long, ByVal wFlag As Long) _
                    As Long
Private mlhHook As Long
Private mlMenuhWnd As Long
Private mfrmCallBack As Form
```

You then need to set up the callback in the Form_Load event.

```
Call InitHook(Me)
```

Then, put the InitHook subroutine in the same modules as those shown in the code I just listed.

```
Public Sub InitHook(CallBackForm As Form)
  Set mfrmCallBack = CallBackForm
  mlMenuhWnd = CallBackForm.hWnd
  mlhHook = SetWindowsHookEx(WH_MSGFILTER, _
                    AddressOf HookMenuProc, _
                        ByVal 0&, _
                    GetWindowThreadProcessId(mlMenuhWnd, _
                      ByVal 0&))
  If mlhHook = 0 Then
    End
  End If
End Sub
```

The InitHook subroutine uses AddressOf to set up a method into which the messages from the Windows message queue are pumped. In this sample code, you are sending the messages to the HookMenuProc subroutine. With the help of the UpdateStatus subroutine in the test Form, the code filters out the message you want and displays help based on the menu item the user's mouse pointer is resting over.

```
Private Function HookMenuProc(ByVal lCode As Long, _
                             ByVal lParam As Long, _
                             mMessage As MSG) As Long
Dim lReturn As Long
Dim lItemID As Long
Dim lItemHandle As Long
Dim lItemFlags As Long
Dim lItemMaxCount As Long
Dim sItemString As String
Dim bMenuDisabled As Boolean
  If lCode = MSGF_MENU Then
    If mMessage.Message = WM_MENUSELECT Then
      lItemHandle = mMessage.lParam
      lItemID = mMessage.wParam And 65535
      lItemFlags = mMessage.wParam / 65535
      If lItemFlags = &HFFFF And lItemHandle = vbNull Then
        sItemString = vbNullString
      Else
        sItemString = Space$(255)
        lItemMaxCount = 255
        If (lItemFlags And MF_POPUP) = MF_POPUP Then
          lReturn = GetMenuString(lItemHandle, lItemID, _
                    sItemString, _
                    lItemMaxCount, MF_BYPOSITION)
        Else
          lReturn = GetMenuString(lItemHandle, lItemID, _
                                  sItemString, lItemMaxCount, _
                                  MF_BYCOMMAND)
        End If
        sItemString = Left$(sItemString, lReturn)
      End If
      If (lItemFlags And MF_DISABLED) = MF_DISABLED Then
        bMenuDisabled = True
      Else
        bMenuDisabled = False
      End If
      mfrmCallBack.UpdateStatus sItemString, bMenuDisabled
```

```
      End If
    End If
  lReturn = CallNextHookEx(mlhHook, lCode, lParam, mMessage)
End Function
```

The code in HookMenuProc is fairly easy to follow. I do need to point out one thing, however. At the end of the subroutine, you are calling the CallNextHookEx API function because you may not be the only one listening to the messages from the Windows message queue; therefore, you need to pass the message along.

The UpdateStatus subroutine should be put in the Form, as follows.

```
Public Sub UpdateStatus(Message As String, MenuDisabled As Boolean)
Dim sDescription As String
  Select Case Message
    Case "&File"
      sDescription = "File menu"
    Case "&New"
      sDescription = "Create a new file"
    Case "&Open..."
      sDescription = "Open a file"
    Case "&Save"
      sDescription = "Save a file"
    Case "S&ave as..."
      sDescription = "Save a file as..."
    Case "&Quit"
      sDescription = "End the application"
    Case "&Edit"
      sDescription = "Edit menu"
    Case "&Cut"
      sDescription = "Cut the text"
    Case "C&opy"
      sDescription = "Copy the text"
    Case "&Paste"
      sDescription = "Paste a text"
    Case Else
      sDescription = vbNullString
  End Select
  If Len(sDescription) > 0 And MenuDisabled Then
    sDescription = "Disabled: " & sDescription
  End If
  StatusBar1.Panels("status").Text = sDescription
End Sub
```

When the Form unloads, you must tell the operating system to stop sending messages. Here is how you do that.

```
Private Sub Form_QueryUnload(Cancel As Integer, _
                             UnloadMode As Integer)
  Call EndHook
End Sub
```

Finally, put the following code in the module file.

```
Public Sub EndHook()
Dim lReturn As Long
  lReturn = UnhookWindowsHookEx(mlhHook)
  Set mfrmCallBack = Nothing
End Sub
```

That's all there is to it. For more information, take a look at the Visual Studio help file for information on AddressOf and other things you can do with the API calls used in this tip.

> **WARNING** *Do not put a break in your code while running in the Visual Basic IDE. If you stop your code at any time whenever you use a message hook, very bad things will happen, such as your entire system locking up. This is primarily due to the fact that you are intercepting messages from the operating system. When your code stops at a break, the messages keep coming to your program and undesirable things can happen. If you want safer message hooking, you might want to get a copy of Spyworks from Desaware (www.desaware.com).*

Detecting whether Your Program Is Running in the Integrated Development Environment

Compatible with: Visual Basic 32-bit
Applies to: Applications

It is often useful to know whether or not a program is running in the Integrated Development Environment (IDE) instead of as a compiled executable. For instance, an error-handling routine can stop a program if an error occurs rather than handle the situation, which would be the case in the compiled version.

The routine for this tip takes advantage of an idiosyncrasy in Visual Basic. All Windows programs must declare a window class for every window. In Visual

Basic, the window class of all Forms is always ThunderForm ("Thunder" was the code name for Visual Basic 1.0). But, the window class for the hidden parent window is different depending on whether the Form is running from the IDE or if it is compiled.

In the IDE, the parent window class is ThunderForm, just as it is with all other Visual Basic windows. In the EXE, however, the class of the parent window is ThunderRT6Form (for Visual Basic 6). Therefore, the IDEMode function will get the window class of the hidden parent window and look for the string RT (which stands for runtime). If the string is found, the program is running as an EXE.

Declare

You'll need to declare the following code in a module file.

```
Public Declare Function GetClassName Lib "user32" Alias _
                        "GetClassNameA" (ByVal hwnd As Long, _
                        ByVal lpClassName As String, _
                        ByVal nMaxCount As Long) As Long
Public Declare Function GetWindowLong Lib "user32" Alias _
                        "GetWindowLongA" (ByVal hwnd As Long, _
                        ByVal nIndex As Long) As Long
Public Const GWL_HWNDPARENT = (-8)
```

Code

Here is the IDEMode function that returns True if the project is running in the IDE.

```
Function IDEMode(FormhWnd As Long) As Boolean
Dim lParent As Long
Dim sClass As String
Dim lReturn As Long
  lParent = GetWindowLong(FormhWnd, GWL_HWNDPARENT)
  sClass = Space$(32)
  lReturn = GetClassName(CLng(lParent), sClass, Len(sClass))
  sClass = Left$(sClass, lReturn)
  Debug.Print sClass
  If InStr(sClass, "RT") Then
    IDEMode = False
    Else
      IDEMode = True
  End If
End Function
```

Example

The following is an example of how to use the IDEMode function.

```
Private Sub Form_Load()
  If IDEMode(Me.hwnd) Then
    MsgBox "IDE detected"
  End If
End Sub
```

You can find the sample code for this tip in the IDEMode.vbp project in the Chapter 9 directory in the downloadable code on the Apress Web site.

Using the SHFormatDrive Function to Format Drives

Compatible with: Visual Basic 32-bit
Applies to: Drives, Windows 95/98, and Windows NT

If you want to provide an easy way for users of your program to format a drive, why not bring up the same Format dialog box that Microsoft Explorer does? (See Figure 9-2.)

To call the Format dialog box, use the SHFormatDrive API function. This function is undocumented by Microsoft (I guess they don't trust us with it). So don't look for any help with this on the Microsoft Development Network CD (although you can find some information on SHFormatDrive for C++ developers in article Q173688 in the Microsoft Knowledge Base). Here, I give you all the information you need to get SHFormatDrive to work properly.

First, take a look at the parameters for SHFormatDrive.

```
Public Declare Function SHFormatDrive Lib "shell32" _
              (ByVal hWnd As Long, ByVal Drive As Long, _
               ByVal fmtID As Long, ByVal Options As Long) _
               As Long
```

- **hWnd**   The Windows handle to the Form from which you are calling this function.

- **Drive**   The drive number that you want to format. Every drive in a computer is assigned a number starting with the A: drive, which is assigned the number 0. Here is an easy way to determine the drive number.

```
lDriveNum = (Asc("A") - 65)
```

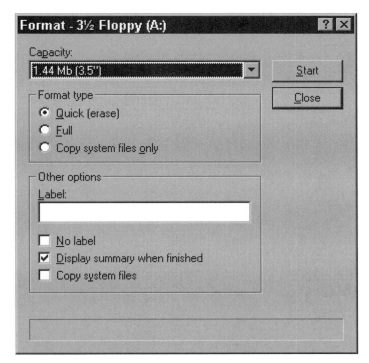

Figure 9-2. The Format dialog box can be called with the
SHFormatDrive *API function*

- **fmtID**   This parameter is used to configure the type of media in the drive. You can set this parameter to work with any type of format, but it is easier to simply let it default to the type of media that is in the drive. Here is constant used to accomplish that.

```
Public Const SHFMT_ID_DEFAULT = &HFFFF
```

- **Options**   The parameter used to configure the type of formatting required for the particular media in the drive. You have the following choices.

```
Public Const SHFMT_OPT_QUICK = &H0 'Quick Format
Public Const SHFMT_OPT_FULL = &H1 'Full Format
Public Const SHFMT_OPT_SYSONLY = &H2 'System Files Only
```

- **Return Values**   If an error occurs, the function returns one of the following values.

```
Public Const SHFMT_NOFORMAT = &HFFFFFFFD
Public Const SHFMT_CANCEL = &HFFFFFFFE
Public Const SHFMT_ERROR = &HFFFFFFFF
```

If an error occurs, a message is displayed to the user.

Example

Here is an example of how to use SHFormatDrive.

```
lReturn = SHFormatDrive(Me.hWnd, lDriveNum, SHFMT_ID_DEFAULT, _
                        SHFMT_OPT_QUICK)
```

Under most circumstances, you should make sure that the drive is removable (most likely it's a floppy drive). You can use the following API call and its constants to do that.

```
Public Const DRIVE_REMOVABLE = 2
Public Const DRIVE_FIXED = 3
Public Const DRIVE_REMOTE = 4
Public Const DRIVE_CDROM = 5
Public Const DRIVE_RAMDISK = 6
Public Declare Function GetDriveType Lib "kernel32" Alias _
                "GetDriveTypeA" (ByVal nDrive As String) _
                As Long
```

You should always use the GetDriveType function and make sure the number returned is 2 before you use the SHFormatDrive function.

You can find the example code for this tip in the FormatDrive.vbp project in the Chapter 9 directory for this book's downloadable code samples (see the Introduction).

> **WARNING** *Be careful when using this code. You could accidentally wipe out your drive or a user's drive if you're not careful!*

Visual Basic Runtime Files

Compatible with: Visual Basic 5 and 6
Applies to: Installations

One question I'm frequently asked at my San Diego Visual Basic Users Group meetings is why a particular program won't work on another computer. Programmers will tell me about e-mailing an executable to someone who can't get it to run. What they may not realize is that for any Visual Basic executable to run, it needs at a minimum the 2MB-plus of the runtime files that get installed with Visual Basic.

Surprise, fear, and horror are just a few of the expressions I see on their faces after I tell them this.

Of course, your programs may need many more files than just the basic Visual Basic runtime files. I could fill an entire chapter on writing good installations (I'll keep that in mind for my next book). If you stick to using the Package and Deployment Wizard that comes with Visual Basic, there isn't much to worry about. It includes all the runtime files Visual Basic requires.

Most seasoned programmers do not use the Package and Deployment Wizard because it's buggy, not very configurable, and slow. The newsgroup traffic in Visual Basic discussion groups would probably drop by 25 percent if Microsoft would stop including it. Most of us turn to a "real" installation package, such as the Wise Installation System (`www.wisesolutions.com`) or InstallShield (`www.installshield.com`). I prefer the Wise Installation System because it's easier to use (and cheaper, too).

If you are creating the install using one of the software programs I just mentioned, you will need a list of the Visual Basic runtime files. The list is also good to have when diagnosing problems on a user's computer. Tables 9-1 and 9-2 list the runtime files and their install settings required for Visual Basic 5 and 6.

Table 9-1. Visual Basic 5 Runtime Files*

FILE NAME	INSTALL SETTINGS
MSVBVM50.DLL	Version Check, Win Shared DLL, Self Register
STDOLE2.TLB	Version Check, TLB Register
OLEAUT32.DLL	Version Check, Win Shared DLL, Self Register
OLEPRO32.DLL	Version Check, Win Shared DLL, Self Register
ASYCFILT.DLL	Version Check, Win Shared DLL, Self Register
CTL3D32.DLL	Version Check
COMCAT.DLL	Version Check, Win Shared DLL, Self Register

*Total Disk Space Required: 2,308,672 bytes

Table 9-2. Visual Basic 6 Runtime Files*

FILE NAME	INSTALL SETTINGS
MSVBVM60.DLL	Version Check, Win Shared DLL, Self Register
STDOLE2.TLB	Version Check, TLB Register
OLEAUT32.DLL	Version Check, Win Shared DLL, Self Register
OLEPRO32.DLL	Version Check, Win Shared DLL, Self Register
ASYCFILT.DLL	Version Check, Win Shared DLL, Self Register
COMCAT.DLL	Version Check, Win Shared DLL, Self Register

*Total Disk Space Required: 2,318,640 bytes

The runtime file sizes may differ on your computer depending on which service pack you have installed on your system. Always try to use the latest Visual Basic service pack available from Microsoft.

The following describes the different Install Settings listed in Tables 9-1 and 9-2.

- **Version Check** The file must be versioned checked. Never install an older version over a newer version and make sure you install the file if the version is the same or older. Why should you install over the same version? Wouldn't it save time if you didn't? Yes, but if the file was somehow corrupted and left the version information intact, then you need to install over it.

- **Win Shared DLL** The file is a Windows Shared DLL. You should mark it as a shared DLL with your install program so that Windows keeps track of how many programs installed that file. Then when an uninstall program tries to remove the file, Windows will warn the user that the file may be used by other programs.

- **Self Register** The file is self-registering.

- **TLB Register** The TLB file needs to be registered. Your install program should provide a way to do this. This step is just as important as registering an executable file.

ActiveX Components and Long File Names

Compatible with: Visual Basic 5 and 6
Applies to: ActiveX (COM) Components

Be especially careful when naming your ActiveX DLL, EXE and OCX files. For example, at my workplace we designed an application (in Visual Basic 5 and C++) and used long file names. For some unexplained reason, we had trouble running the COM objects after registering them in the Registration Database. We switched to the old 8.3 file names and the problem went away.

I could not find any official information about this in the Microsoft Knowledge Base. But, if you look, all COM components released by Microsoft use 8.3 file names. Go figure.

Registering and Unregistering COM Objects Easily

Compatible with: All COM (ActiveX) Objects
Applies to: DLLs, OCXs, EXEs

After you create COM (ActiveX) objects in Visual Basic or have used other COM objects in your projects, you will need to register and unregister those objects, for a number of reasons. For instance, you may need to manually install COM objects or you may need to register or unregister objects for testing purposes. I'll bet most of you do this by choosing Start ➔ Run and typing in regsvr32 and the file name and path of the file you want to register, or typing in regsvr32 /u and the file name and path of the file you want to unregister.

Wouldn't you rather register an object by right-clicking the file name in Explorer? (See Figure 9-3.) You can by simply adding some entries into the Registration Database.

Instead of going into a lengthy explanation of how to do this, I have provided some .reg files that enable you to easily add the appropriate entries in the

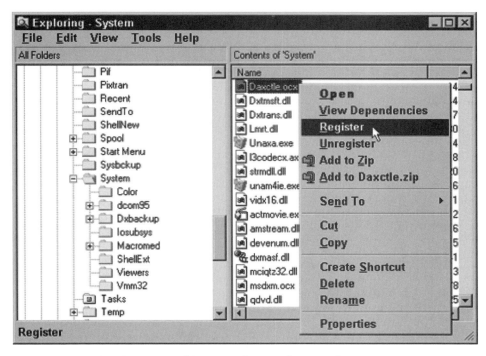

Figure 9-3. Registering COM objects via the Windows Explorer

Registration Database. You can find the following .reg files in the Chapter 9 directory in the downloadable code for this book on the Apress Web site (see the Introduction).

- **regunregexe.reg**   Adds the appropriate entries to register and unregister EXE files.

- **regunregdll.reg**   Adds the appropriate entries to register and unregister DLL files.

- **regunregocx.reg**   Adds the appropriate entries to register and unregister OCX files.

To add the entries, simply double-click the reg file of your choice.

CHAPTER 10

Miscellaneous but Nevertheless Super-Useful Tips

THE TIPS IN THIS CHAPTER DON'T EASILY FIT into any of the other chapters, so they ended up here in this miscellaneous collection, which is not to say they are any less useful than the other tips in this book. You'll discover a cool way to change the MousePointer, find tips on files you need to distribute with your Visual Basic application, learn how to disable Dr. Watson, and more.

I end this chapter with a tip that seems appropriate for the close of this book: How do you bring the Visual Basic IDE back to its pristine original state if your windows have docked in strange places and nothing seems to be right in the IDE anymore?

Changing the MousePointer with Class

Compatible with: Visual Basic 32-bit
Applies to: Applications

When performing long operations in your program, it's always good to change the MousePointer to an hourglass (or whatever pointer you want) so that the user does not start wildly clicking on your program thinking that it has locked up. At the beginning of a long operation, be sure to change the MousePointer, and remember to change it back when the operation is done.

But what if an error occurs before you change the MousePointer back? And what if you forget to change it back (and QA sends your code back to you)?

Here is an easy way to set the MousePointer and not have to worry about setting it back. All you need to do is to wrap up the following code in a Class. First, create the Class as an object, set the MousePointer, and then when the object goes out of scope (that is, when the method ends) Visual Basic will destroy the object. In the Terminate event of the Class, you just set the MousePointer back to whatever it was. Very cool!

Just follow these steps:

1. Create a new Class in your project and name it `clsMousePointer`.

2. Next, place the following code in it.

```
Private lOrigPointer As Long
Private vUseObject As Variant
Public Sub SetCursor(Optional UseObject As Variant, _
                        Optional Pointer As Variant)
Dim lNewPointer As Long
On Error Resume Next
  'Save the current cursor
  If IsMissing(UseObject) Then
    lOrigPointer = Screen.MousePointer
    Else
      lOrigPointer = UseObject.MousePointer
      Set vUseObject = UseObject
  End If
  'Default to Hourglass
  lNewPointer = vbHourglass
  If Not IsMissing(Pointer) Then
    If IsNumeric(Pointer) Then
      'Substitute with your own pointer if needed
      lNewPointer = Pointer
    End If
  End If
  'Set the pointer
  If IsMissing(UseObject) Then
    Screen.MousePointer = lNewPointer
    Else
      UseObject.MousePointer = lNewPointer
  End If
End Sub
Private Sub Class_Terminate()
On Error Resume Next
  'Restore pointer
  If IsEmpty(vUseObject) Then
    Screen.MousePointer = lOrigPointer
  Else
    vUseObject.MousePointer = lOrigPointer
  End If
End Sub
```

Example

Here is an example of how to use the `clsMousePointer` Class.

```
Private Sub Command1_Click()
Dim lCounter As Long
Dim MousePointer As New clsMousePointer
  MousePointer.SetCursor Command1, vbCrosshair
  'Long Operation goes here.
End Sub
```

After the "long operation" ends and the Sub exits, the reference to `MousePointer` goes out of scope. Therefore, the `Terminate` event for it will be called (restoring the mouse pointer back to its original state).

The neat thing about the `SetCursor` method in `clsMousePointer` is that you can send any object to the method that supports the `MousePointer` property (such as a Form, ComboBox, ListBox, and such). By default, this method uses the Screen object. In the second parameter, you can set the method to any valid `MousePointer` value (such as `vbCrosshair`). By default, it changes the `MousePointer` of the object to an hourglass (`vbHourGlass`).

You can find code for this class in the clsMousePointer.cls file in the Chapter 10 directory in the downloadable code from the Apress Web site (see the Introduction for more information).

Converting Hours to Minutes

Compatible with: All versions of Visual Basic
Applies to: Time

The following quick tip demonstrates how to write a function that converts hours to minutes. It also shows you how to write a function that converts minutes to hours and minutes.

```
Function ConvertMinsHours(TimeValue As String) As String
Dim lTemp As Long
Dim lHour As Long
Dim lMinute As Long
Dim lPos As Long
  lPos = Val(InStr(TimeValue, ":"))
  If lPos = 0 Then
    lTemp = Val(TimeValue)
    lHour = 0
```

```
      If lTemp >= 60 Then
        lHour = Int(lTemp / 60)
      End If
      lMinute = lTemp - (lHour * 60)
      ConvertMinsHours = Format$(lHour, "#0") + ":" + _
                         Format$(lMinute, "00")
    Else
        lHour = Val(Left$(TimeValue, InStr(TimeValue, ":") - 1))
        lMinute = Val(Mid$(TimeValue, InStr(TimeValue, ":") + 1, _
                       Len(TimeValue)))
        ConvertMinsHours = CStr((lHour * 60) + lMinute)
  End If
End Function
```

Example

Here are a couple of examples of the ConvertMinsHours function. Use the following code to convert hours to minutes.

```
sMintues = ConvertMinsHours("12:00")
```

This code then returns

```
720
```

Use the following code to convert minutes to hours and minutes.

```
sMintues = ConvertMinsHours("345")
```

This code will then return

```
5:45
```

Displaying 3D Text without a Control

Compatible with: All versions of Visual Basic
Applies to: Form, Text

This very simple procedure allows you to print text in 3D, without an OCX or API call. You just need to specify where the text will be printed and the size of the shadow.

Figure 10-1. An example of 3D text on a Form

First, you need to set up the form, as follows.

1. On your Form, set the AutoRedraw to True and the ScaleMode to
    3 - Pixel.

2. Change the Font and Font Size to whatever you want.

3. Add following code to the Form_Load() event.

```
Private Sub Form_Load()
Dim iShadowX As Integer
Dim iShadowY As Integer
Dim iCounter As Integer
  Me.Show
  Me.Cls
  'Set Scalemode to pixel
  Me.ScaleMode = 3
  'Change the Forecolor of Form to Shadow Color (Dark grey)
  Me.ForeColor = "&H808080"
  'Set The Top of the Shadow
  iShadowY = 5
  'Set The Left of the Shadow
  iShadowX = 5
  For iCounter = 0 To 5
    Me.CurrentX = iShadowX + iCounter
    Me.CurrentY = iShadowY + iCounter
    If iCounter = 5 Then
      'Change the Color to White
      Me.ForeColor = vbWhite
    End If
    Me.Print "VB Tips & Tricks!"
  Next
End Sub
```

You can find the sample code for this tip in the ShadowText.vbp project in the downloadable code for Chapter 10 (see the Introduction).

Fixing the "License Information for This Component Not Found" Error

Compatible with: Visual Basic 5
Applies to: Components

When using some of the controls that come with Visual Basic 5.0, you may get the following error:

License Information For This Component Not Found. You Do Not Have An Appropriate License To Use This Functionality In The Design Environment.

This can make you pretty darn angry. You paid for Visual Basic 5, so why can't you use the control? Simply put, Microsoft admitted to me that a problem exists with the install that causes the license information to not be entered into the Registration Database under certain circumstances.

Microsoft has published a fix for this. You need to download the following program:

```
http://support.microsoft.com/download/support/mslfiles/Vbc.exe
```

When you run this program, it will fix the license information problem you may be having with any of the following controls:

Auto Connection Manager (AddIn)
Microsoft Tabbed Dialog Control
Microsoft Winsock Control
Microsoft Comm Control
Microsoft RemoteData Control
Microsoft Common Dialog Control
Microsoft Data Bound Grid Control
Microsoft Windows Common Controls (1)
Microsoft PictureClip Control
Microsoft Flexgrid Control
Microsoft Internet Transfer Control
Microsoft Chart Control
Microsoft MAPI Controls
Microsoft Windows Common Controls (2)
VB T-SQL Debugger (AddIn)
Microsoft Remote Data Object 2.0

Microsoft Multimedia Control
Microsoft Masked Edit Control
Microsoft Rich TextBox Control
Microsoft SysInfo Control

For more information, see article Q181854 in the Microsoft Technical Knowledge Base. If Microsoft ever removes this program from its Web site, you can download it from the VB Tips & Tricks Web site (see Appendix A). I also included the Vbc.exe file in the file you can download from the Apress Web site.

Disabling Dr. Watson on Windows NT

Compatible with: Windows NT
Applies to: Dr. Watson

When you're in the Visual Basic IDE and running your code, a Dr. Watson error occasionally may occur on Windows NT. Whenever this happens to me, I get so many message boxes that my system slows to a crawl. It can take me up to five minutes to get to the Task Manager and End Task on Dr. Watson.

A better way exists to deal with this annoyance—you can prevent it from ever coming up. The Microsoft Knowledgebase suggests using the following steps to disable Dr. Watson (article Q188296).

1. Select Start ➔ Run, enter `regedit.exe` in the Open edit box, and click OK.

2. Locate the following registry key:

    `HKEY_LOCAL_MACHINE\Software\Microsoft\Windows NT\CurrentVersion\AeDebug`

3. Click the AeDebug key, and then click Export Registry File on the Registry menu.

4. Enter a name and location for the saved registry file, and click Save.

5. Delete the AeDebug key.

> **NOTE** *Steps 3 and 4 are optional, unless you want to restore the default use of Dr. Watson.*

If you want to enable Dr. Watson, just use these steps.

1. At a command prompt, enter the following:

    ```
    drwtsn32 -I
    ```

2. Press Enter.

3. Double-click the .reg file you previously created in steps 3 and 4.

Running Programs at Startup

Compatible with: Windows 32-bit
Applies to: Computer Startup

If you want a particular program to run automatically when Windows starts, instead of creating a shortcut in the Startup menu, you can make the following Registration Database entries. Just use these steps:

1. Locate the following key.

    ```
    HKEY_LOCAL_MACHINE\Software\Microsoft\Windows\CurrentVersion\Run
    ```

2. Add a new string value. You can give the value any name, but typically the name of the program is used.

3. Double-click the new value and type in the path, file name, and any command line parameters. For example,

    ```
    Value Name = Notepad
    Value Data = c:\windows\notepad.exe
    ```

If you want to run programs when loading a user, follow the same steps but use this key instead.

```
HKEY_CURRENT_USER\Software\Microsoft\Windows\CurrentVersion\Run
```

This may be a good thing to do during your program installation.

Discovering the COMCTL32.OCX, COMCT232.OCX, MSChart.OCX Controls Upgrades

Compatible with: Visual Basic 6
Applies to: COMCTL32.OCX, COMCT232.OCX, MSChart.OCX Controls

After upgrading your projects from Visual Basic 5 to Visual Basic 6, you might notice that the comctl32.ocx, comct232.ocx, and mschart.ocx controls still say that they are version 5.0 (SP2).

At first, I thought that Microsoft hadn't updated these controls, but I was wrong. Microsoft did update them, while also changing their file names and interfaces, but did not automatically update the controls as was done in previous versions of Visual Basic.

Here are the new file names for the controls.

comctl32.ocx is now mscomctl.ocx.
comct232.ocx is now mscomct2.ocx.
mschart.ocx is now mschrt20.ocx.

I worked for hours to "manually" convert my projects over to the new "6.0" control versions. No matter what I did, the projects would not run after I updated them and fixed the interface changes. I would only receive an error from Visual Basic, which was no help at all (thanks a lot Microsoft).

After searching the Microsoft site, I found the answer. Microsoft came up with an upgrade utility (ActiveX Control Upgrade Utility) that will automatically scan a project and make the appropriate changes. It is easy to use and works perfectly. To get more information on this utility and download it, go to

```
http://msdn.microsoft.com/vbasic/downloads/axupgrade.asp
```

You can also download the program that fixes this problem from the VB Tips & Tricks Web site (see Appendix A). I also put the utility (ProjUpgd.EXE) in the Chapter 10 folder in the downloadable code for this book.

Getting the Screen Resolution

Compatible with: All versions of Visual Basic
Applies to: Screens

Here is a quick tip on how to determine the current screen resolution. I use this most often in my screensaver programs. It is also a must if you have to make a program's UI conform to the user's screen resolution.

Code

Place the following code in a module.

```
Public Type ScreenRes
  Width As Long
  Height As Long
End Type
Public Function GetScreenRes() As ScreenRes
Dim lXTwips As Long
Dim lYTwips As Long
Dim lXPixels As Long
Dim lYPixels As Long
  lXTwips = Screen.TwipsPerPixelX
  lYTwips = Screen.TwipsPerPixelY
  lYPixels = Screen.Height / lYTwips
  lXPixels = Screen.Width / lXTwips
  GetScreenRes.Height = lYPixels
  GetScreenRes.Width = lXPixels
End Function
```

Example

The following example demonstrates how to use the GetScreenRes function.

```
Dim srScreenRes As ScreenRes
  srScreenRes = GetScreenRes()
  Debug.Print srScreenRes.Width
  Debug.Print srScreenRes.Height
```

Determining Who's Logged onto the Computer

Compatible with: Windows NT

Have you ever needed to know the name of the user who is currently logged onto a computer, in addition to the computer name? It takes just a few mouse clicks to get this information. And, wouldn't it be nice to have the My Computer icon display this information? Well, you can accomplish this with just a few modifications to the Registration Database. The following steps show you how.

Figure 10-2. A My Computer icon showing the name of the user who's currently logged on and the computer name

1. Start the Registry Editor (regedt32.exe). You can't use regedit.exe to do this (I learned the hard way).

2. Go to the following key:

    `HKEY_CLASSES_ROOT\CLSID\{20D04FE0-3AEA-1069-A2D8-08002B30309D}`

3. From the Edit menu, select Add Value.

4. Leave the value name blank and set the type to REG_EXPAND_SZ

5. Click OK and enter **User: %USERNAME% on: %COMPUTERNAME%.**

6. Click OK and close the Registry Editor.

7. Click the Desktop and press F5. You should now see something similar to Figure 10-2.

That's all there is to it. Unfortunately, this works only with Windows NT. *Attention all quality assurance people:* To make programmers happy that they do not have to ask for the name of a machine, please use this tip!

Invoking the Windows Shortcut Wizard

Compatible with: Visual Basic 32-bit
Applies to: Applications

This tip shows you how to call the Windows 95/98 or Windows NT Shortcut Wizard to create a shortcut to a specific directory for any file the user may want (as shown in Figure 10-3). When the Shortcut Dialog box comes up, users can use it to make a link to a file.

This is great for applications that use shortcuts, plus you can keep them all in one place.

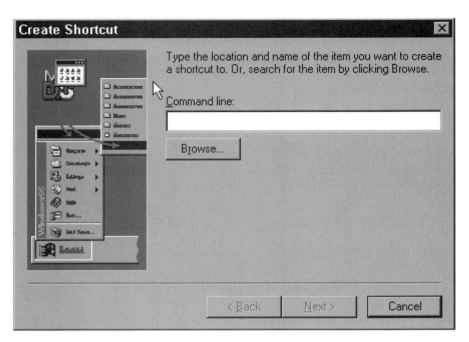

Figure 10-3. The Windows Shortcut Wizard dialog

```
Private Sub Command1_Click()
Dim lReturn As Long
  lReturn = Shell("rundll32.exe AppWiz.Cpl,NewLinkHere " & _
                  App.Path & "\", vbNormalFocus)
End Sub
```

> **NOTE** *The previous two tips can also be coded very easily using the new Microsoft Shell Automation Objects that come in Windows 2000 and can be downloaded for any 32-bit version of Windows. These objects are worth checking out!*

Fixing the "Could not be Loaded" Error

Compatible with: Visual Basic 6
Applies to: Applications

The "Could not be Loaded" error typically occurs when you're trying to reference a Visual Basic ActiveX OCX. The error is caused by the OLE Class ID changing in your ActiveX project while the GUID does not change. I see this happening mostly in Visual Basic 6.

I just happen to have a solution to this problem: Run RegClean or remove all references to your ActiveX OCX in the Registration Database, and then re-register your OCX.

You can find the RegClean program (regclean.exe) in the Chapter 10 directory of this book's downloadable code.

> **WARNING**   *Microsoft has periodically removed RegClean from its Web site because it can damage your Registration Database (although I have used it for years with no problems). The current version can be found at http://support.microsoft.com/support/downloads/DP3049.ASP. In any case, exercise caution when using RegClean!*

Fixing the "Can't find project or library" Compile Error

Compatible with: Visual Basic 6
Applies to: Applications

The "Can't find project or library" compile error is by far the most common of the worthless errors I've encountered in Visual Basic. When you see this error in the design window, it will look something like Figure 10-4.

In Figure 10-4, Trim$ seems to be part of the VBA object, so how could it be missing? Actually, it's not. Another reference in the project is missing. If you click OK, you should see the References dialog box (shown in Figure 10-5).

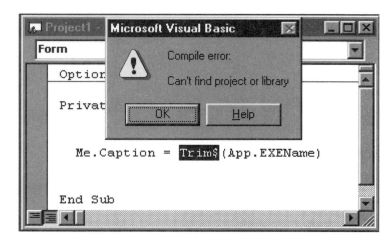

Figure 10-4. The error message in action

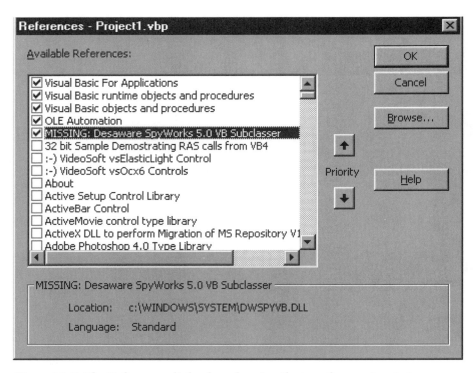

Figure 10-5. The References dialog box showing that a reference is missing

This indicates that an object, which you may or may not be using, is not referenced on the machine.

This problem has a solution: First, deselect the MISSING reference. If you need this reference in your project, you'll have to find the new reference to it. If you can't find the new reference, then you have to install or re-register the file for that object.

Restoring the Visual Basic IDE Back to Its Original State

Compatible with: Visual Basic 6

One annoying aspect of Visual Basic is that Microsoft left out a method to restore the Visual Basic IDE back to its original state, which is shown in Figure 10-6.

This is especially bothersome because the docking feature of Visual Basic can make windows stick to places you would never ever want them to be.

The UI and DOCK features of Visual Basic are controlled by two keys in the registry. If you delete them manually via Regedit or programmatically, the next

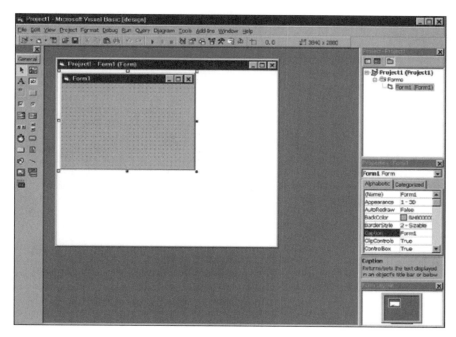

Figure 10-6. The original Visual Basic IDE

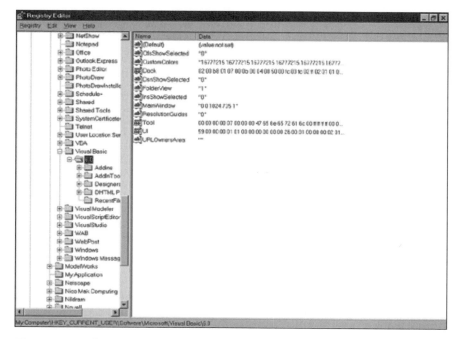

Figure 10-7. The Regedit screen for the Visual Basic UI in the default installation

time Visual Basic starts up it will use the default values for docking and the UI, thereby bringing the Windows in the Visual Basic IDE back to their original state. Those two keys that control the UI and DOCK features are

```
HKEY_CURRENT_USER\Software\Microsoft\Visual Basic\6.0\UI
```

and

```
HKEY_CURRENT_USER\Software\Microsoft\Visual Basic\6.0\Dock
```

Figure 10-7 shows you the registry values for a default installation of Visual Basic 6 inside Regedit.

APPENDIX A

Touring the VB Tips & Tricks Web Site

THE VB TIPS & TRICKS SITE (`www.vbtt.com`) is chockfull of comprehensive information on the topic of Visual Basic, including all the tips, tricks, articles, and reviews published in the *VB Tips & Tricks* newsletter since it began publishing. The site even has a search engine to make it easier to find what you need.

I maintain the VB Tips & Tricks Web site, while the guys at Spider Eye Studios have been nice enough to host the site for me for about two years now. Most of the tips and articles on the site come from programmers just like you who want to share their knowledge with others.

By visiting the site you can find out how to win free software, books, and other stuff (more on that later). This appendix lists some of the highlights of the site, but feel free to check it out yourself.

VB Tips & Tricks Newsletter

The VB Tips & Tricks Web site is home to the *VB Tips & Tricks* newsletter. The newsletter was launched in September 1993 as a one-stop shopping place for Visual Basic programmers looking for information on the programming language. As of February 1999, the newsletter has been a totally free Web-based publication, and it will stay that way.

Programming Tips

Click on the **Programming Tips** link and here you can link to areas of the site called the Beginners Corner, Visual Basic for Windows, Visual Basic for Windows CE, Visual Basic and The Internet, Visual Basic & MS Access, Windows Help Files, Windows 32-bit, and others. Most of the tips on using Visual Basic can be found under these sections.

Advanced Programming Techniques

Under the **Advanced Programming Techniques** link is a section designed for beginning to intermediate programmers who want to move to the next level of Visual Basic programming. Areas of interest here include the links to Advanced Programming Articles and Application Installations.

The advanced news articles are typically longer and more involved than the site's tips and require a greater understanding of the intricacies of Visual Basic and Windows. Many of the articles focus on the more-advanced aspects of Windows API calls.

Software Development

Click on the **Software Development** link and you'll find information on advanced subjects that programmers deal with in their everyday jobs. The topics include Visual Basic and Globalization, Legal Issues (such as copyright infringement and software development agreements), and other subjects.

Component Products and Reviews

Because add-on components constitute such a large market (and what partly lead to the huge popularity of Visual Basic), and because we all eventually use them in our projects, an entire section of the Web site is dedicated to add-on components. You'll find links to Component Reviews, Books/ Newsletter/ Magazine Reviews, Component Listings, Component Tips & Tricks, Bug Watch, VB Tips & Tricks Reader Choice Awards, Top 10 Component Products, and the latest component news in the News Flash section.

Many programmers are fans of the Bug Watch section, which lists component bugs found by VB Tips & Tricks readers and me. Visual Basic bugs are also listed, plus any known solutions.

Be sure to check out the VB Tips & Tricks Reader Choice Awards and Top 10 Component Products to get a scoop on the best Visual Basic components. In short, be sure to check out this section of the site before you purchase any Visual Basic component.

VB Dave's Corner

This is my own personal spot on the VB Tips & Tricks Web site. Here, I list my choices for the best Visual Basic components and the best programming books.

Just click the **Favorite Programming Books** link. Then, click the cover graphic for any book and you'll be whisked to the Amazon.com page for that book. Keep an eye on this page for my latest picks.

My favorite feature of VB Dave's Corner is called Worthless VB Errors. I list those funky errors that Visual Basic gives you that seem to make no sense whatsoever, and explain what causes these puzzling errors and their solutions.

VB Tips & Tricks Report Cards

If your experiences are anything like mine, it's not uncommon for your boss to walk into your office and tell you that the program you are currently working on needs a new feature added to it right away (which really means yesterday!).

Because so many vendors are creating components for Visual Basic, it's sometimes hard for a developer to pick and choose from among them. You don't have spare days or weeks to research a component that will work the way you want it to, so you paw through your stack of magazines and marketing materials and make the best choice in the few hours you have.

Marketing materials will tell you about a component's features, but not how good it really is. Magazine reviews are better, but most of the time they are written by programmers or editors who have used the component for just a few days— not nearly long enough to tell you how the component truly works in a real-life project.

This is where the VB Tips & Tricks Report Card comes in handy. Programmers like you submit a grade on a component (and can change their grade at any time). And, like you, they have used the component for longer than just a few days and in real-world projects. They have a first-hand knowledge of how the component actually performs.

VB Tips & Tricks Report Cards give you the opportunity to broadcast your feelings about a component while providing *the* resource for choosing a good component. Although no selection method guarantees that a component will be the absolute best one for a project, this is a good place to start.

To encourage programmers to grade components, participants are automatically entered to win some cool software we give away each month.

Using Report Cards to Grade Products

The VB Tips & Tricks Report Cards make it easy for you to grade a component. Simply go to the **Submit a Report Card** page. There you can submit a Report Card on more than 600 Visual Basic-related components, books, magazines, and Web sites. You can grade a product on its suitability for a task, how technically sound it is, its ease of use, its documentation, and more, and then give it your final grade.

An entry field enables you to let other programmers know what you liked or disliked about a product and another field allows you to enter suggestions on how to make a product better. Those suggestions are e-mailed directly to the vendors.

What Happens to the Information You Submit

After your Report Card is submitted, it is entered into a database and the following pages are created from that information:

- A Top 10 Components page that lists the top-ten products based on their final grades and the number of Report Cards submitted for that product.

- A Bottom 10 Components page that lists the lowest-graded products.

- An All Components Grades page that is enormously valuable for programmers looking for a good component. Here you can select a category (such as Development Tools, Internet Products, and others) and you'll see every product that's been graded. This should be the place to start your search for a new product.

The Report Card shows you how the product was graded, how many programmers graded the product, information about the product, and the company that makes it (see Figure A-1).

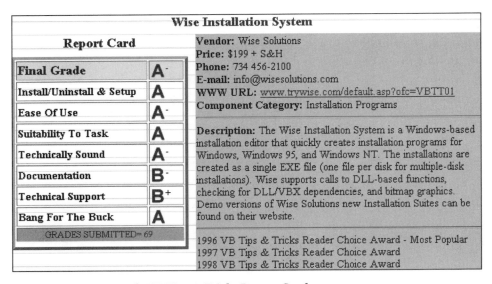

Figure A-1. An example VB Tips & Tricks Report Card

Free Software Contest, Downloads, and More

Many more areas of interest can be found on the VB Tips & Tricks Web site and you can explore them for yourself. I should mention that whenever you submit tips, articles, bugs, or Worthless VB Errors to the site, you're entered in a monthly contest to win some really cool software, books, and other stuff. You'll also find a download area to obtain all the sample code and programs from the site's tips and articles.

What makes the VB Tips & Tricks Web site so influential is that programmers like you and I write it. VB Tips & Tricks is the vehicle that lets everyone share his or her collective programming knowledge.

APPENDIX B

Visual Basic Information Resources

SO MUCH INFORMATION EXISTS ON just about every aspect of Visual Basic that it can be difficult to find exactly what you need, when you need it. This appendix is designed to steer you to some essential Visual Basic resources. In addition to the top Visual Basic Web sites, I've listed some of my favorite Visual Basic publications, newsgroups, and other helpful information.

Web Sites

Numerous Web sites are devoted to the topic of Visual Basic, but few have any really good, solid content. Most are just links to better Visual Basic Web sites, or to other bad sites (a real waste of Internet space). Among the good Visual Basic sites, the following are my favorites. (My very own VB Tips & Tricks Web site is featured in Appendix A.)

Microsoft Visual Basic Home Page

msdn.microsoft.com/vbasic/

This is the official Visual Basic site from Microsoft. I must hand it to Microsoft, over the past year or two they've really added to the amount of valuable information available on the site.

In previous years, there wasn't much to see here outside of Visual Basic service packs. Microsoft is now offering product overviews and demos, technical information, and news and reviews (including their VB Tips & Tricks Reader Choice Award). You'll also find a **Samples & Downloads** link to Visual Basic sample programs, utilities, Visual Basic add-ins, and more.

I check out this site at least once a week to keep abreast of the latest official Visual Basic news and service packs.

Carl & Gary's Visual Basic Home Page

www.cgvb.com/

One of the original, non-commercial, not-for-profit Visual Basic Web sites is Carl & Gary's Visual Basic Home Page. These guys have always had one of the best selections of Visual Basic–related links and component vendor information. The site also has information on user groups, Internet programming, and more. They even have a **Humor** link to jokes, spoofs, and other funny stuff (which we all need once in a while).

DevX—The Development Exchange

www.devx.com/

This site is produced by Fawcette Technical Publications, publisher of the *Visual Basic Programmers Journal.* Here you will find feature articles, news, tips, and other items that have appeared in the pages of the magazine. You can also purchase Visual Basic components and books from this site.

This site is also the online home to other Fawcette technical publications on programming technologies and topics such as Java, XML, Web development, C++, and more.

VBWire

vbwire.com/

VBWire is your one-stop destination for the latest news from the Visual Basic world. Anyone can post news here, so the information about just-released products and related Web sites is endless. You don't even have to remember to check the Web site every day. VBWire will send the news to you via e-mail! You'll also find useful tips and a chat room where you can talk to fellow programmers.

VBNet—The Visual Basic Developers Resource Centre

www.mvps.org/vbnet/

This site is loaded with lots of good tips that deal mostly with the Windows API. This site also features code samples, a code library, and links to worthwhile reference books. You'll also find numerous links to other sites and a FAQ library.

Publications

The following titles should be on just about every Visual Basic programmer's bookshelf. You can purchase any of these books through the VB Tips & Tricks Online Web site (see Appendix A for more information).

Dan Appleman's Visual Basic Programmer's Guide to the Win32 API

by Daniel Appleman (Sams)

This is the number-one book that all Visual Basic programmers need. You will undoubtedly program to the Windows API some day, and this book is the single best reference on the subject. You need this book, so buy it now!

Doing Objects in Microsoft Visual Basic 6

by Deborah Kurata (QUE)

If you are a Visual Basic novice or new to object-oriented programming, this is the book for you. Deborah Kurata explains the methodology behind object-oriented programming (OOP), how to apply it, and how to use it in Visual Basic 6. This is the best book on the market about OOP that targets Visual Basic.

Visual Basic 6.0 Internet Programming

by Carl Franklin (John Wiley & Sons, Inc.)

This newly revised title on Visual Basic and Internet programming is authored by Carl Franklin, the Visual Basic world's Internet guru. Franklin started working with and writing about Internet programming before most programmers even knew what it was. He speaks on the topic at the Visual Basic Insiders Technical Summit, writes related articles for the *Visual Basic Programmers Journal*, and has even written the coolest Internet-based training program around, called WorldTrain.

This book is the sum of Franklin's many years of programming with Visual Basic for the Internet. He explains Winsock programming, E-mail programming, and much more.

About Face: The Essentials of User Interface Design

by Alan Cooper (IDG Books Worldwide, Inc.)

Alan Cooper has been called "The Father of Visual Basic." From what I've heard, he wrote the first Visual Basic prototype and sold it to our friend Bill Gates. Cooper is now into user interfaces, and this book is a must have!

Cooper can help you write a better interface, which is a *very* important piece of your programs. He is also just about the best speaker I have ever had the pleasure of hearing. If you can, catch him at the next Visual Basic Insiders Technical Summit. His presentation alone will be well worth the ticket price.

Visual Basic Programmers Journal

This magazine has always been the best single periodical for Visual Basic programmers. It is published monthly, with some extra issues thrown in during the year. It is also available on CD-ROM. You can subscribe to it by visiting the DevX Web site at www.devx.com.

User Groups

Another fantastic place to get help is through your local Visual Basic user group. I help run the user group here in San Diego and we host an average of 70 to 100 programmers each month, ranging from experts to those who haven't even bought their first copy of Visual Basic.

Find the Visual Basic user group nearest you and get involved. You won't regret it. It was through my work in helping to run the San Diego group that I found my last three full-time jobs and eventually tripled my salary! The Carl & Gary's Visual Basic Home Page (mentioned earlier in this appendix) has a **User Groups** link to an excellent list of groups.

Newsgroups

Newsgroups provide a means to post questions online in order to get a response from someone who hopefully knows the answer. Here, I've noted my favorite Visual Basic newsgroup, and a resource that lists many others.

NOTE *To participate in a newsgroup, you first need a program that can read messages and respond to them. You could, of course, write such a program in Visual Basic, but many easy-to-use, fantastic newsreader programs are already available. They include Microsoft Outlook Express, Netscape Message Center, and Agent from Forté, Inc.*

news.devx.com

The DevX Discussions newsgroup is hosted by Fawcette Technical Publications, publisher of the *Visual Basic Programmers Journal*. Naturally, this is my favorite newsgroup because it's moderated by fellow writers for the magazine and myself. These writers are the top Visual Basic programmers in the country and they answer a good majority of the questions. Discussion groups center around topics such as databases, control creation, object-oriented programming, Windows API, VBA, and many other subjects.

msnews.microsoft.com

This is Microsoft's newsgroup server that, as of this writing, had 1,068 discussion groups. Because this server is sponsored by Microsoft, these groups are very active. And, occasionally, someone from Microsoft will take the time to answer questions. The discussion groups tackle topics including Web development, third-party components, databases, installations, Windows API, and more.

Visual Basic Insiders Technical Summit

The publisher of the invaluable *Visual Basic Programmers Journal* hosts the biggest Visual Basic conference in the world, the Visual Basic Insiders Technical Summit. The summit's events run for several days and are jam-packed with sessions to teach you just about everything that Visual Basic can do. The sessions are taught by people from Microsoft, writer-editors from the journal, and the top Visual Basic reporters. If you can get your company to foot the bill, this is an event you should not miss.

The largest of these conferences takes place in San Francisco, usually in February or March of each year. That's the one I'll be attending. To learn more about these conferences, head to www.devx.com.

Microsoft Developers Network

The Microsoft Developers Network (MSDN) is the official Microsoft-sponsored source for comprehensive programming information, development toolkits, and testing platforms. MSDN delivers all of this via a quarterly subscription, so you can be confident that you're always working with the most up-to-date information and technology.

Each quarter, you can receive all the Microsoft documentation on CD-ROM, the latest versions of all the different flavors of Windows, and a whole lot more. It's a little costly, but well worth it, and a must for any development shop. In fact, I would never work for a company that does not subscribe to it. You can find out more by going to MSDN Online at `msdn.microsoft.com`.

You can also get biweekly information (including the latest resources, service packs, SDKs, betas, and new products) via e-mail if you go to the MSDN Web site and click on **MSDN Online Flash**.

The APIGID32.DLL Library

THE FUNCTIONS DESCRIBED IN THIS APPENDIX are part of the apigid32.dll dynamic link library. This DLL, provided by Desaware, contains a number of routines that should prove useful when working with API functions. The source code for this library can be found on the Apress Web site. You may distribute the DLL with your compiled Visual Basic applications. However, Desaware does not provide free support for this DLL.

Numeric Functions

The following functions operate on numeric variables, providing features that are difficult to implement in Visual Basic due to its lack of unsigned data types.

agDWORDto2Integers

```
Declare Function agDWORDto2Integers lib "apigid32.dll" (ByVal l As long,
lw As _ Integer,
```

Many Windows API functions return a long variable that contains two integers. This function provides an efficient way to separate the two integers. The value passed in parameter l is divided, with the low 16 bits loaded into the lw parameter and the high 16 bits loaded into the lh parameter.

agPOINTStoLong

```
Declare Function agPOINTStolong lib "apigid32.dll" (pt As POINTS) As Long
```

Converts a POINTS structure into a Long, placing the X field in the low 16 bits of the result and the Y field in the high 16 bits of the result. This function is convenient for Windows API functions that expect POINTS structures to be passed as Long parameters.

agSwapBytes, agSwapWords

```
Declare Function agSwapBytes Lib "apigid32.dll" (ByVal src As Integer) As Integer
Declare Function agSwapWords Lib "apigid32.dll" (ByVal src As Long) As Long
```

In rare situations, you may need to swap the order of bytes in an integer or the integers in a long. This will typically occur when working with file formats defined originally for non-Intel processors. This function provides an easy way to accomplish this task.

Pointer and Buffer Routines

These functions can be helpful when handling certain types of string and buffer operations. The operation of these functions can be implemented using Visual Basic alone. However, these functions can be more efficient and are easier to use.

agCopyData, agCopyDataBynum

```
Declare Sub agCopyData Lib "apigid32.dll" (source As Any, dest As Any, ByVal _
nCount As long)
Declare Sub agCopyDataBynum Lib "apigid32.dll" Alias "agCopyData" (ByVal _
source As Long, ByVal dest As Long, ByVal nCount As Long)
```

This function is provided to copy data from one object to another. Two forms of this function are provided. The first accepts any type of object. If the two objects were of the same type, you could simply use the Visual Basic LSet function. However, this function can be used for copying only the specified part of the object.

The second form accepts Long parameters. It is typically used to copy data between Visual Basic structures and string buffers or memory blocks.

The source parameter specifies the address of the start of a block of memory to copy.

The dest parameter specifies the destination address for the data.

The nCount parameter specifies the number of bytes to copy.

The RtlMoveMemory function performs the same task and is used extensively in this book. Note, however, that the order of source and destination parameters is reversed in the two functions.

Make sure that the parameters for this function are valid and that the entire range specified by nCount is also valid.

agGetAddressForObject, agGetAddressForInteger, agGetAddressForLong, agGetAddressForLPSTR, agGetAddressForVBString

```
Declare Function agGetAddressForObject Lib "apigid32.dll" (object As Any) As Long
Declare Function agGetAddressForInteger Lib "apigid32.dll" Alias _
"agGetAddressForObject" (intnum As Integer) As Long
Declare Function agGetAddressForLong Lib "apigid32.dll" Alias _
"agGetAddressForObject" (intnum As Long) As Long
Declare Function agGetAddressForVBString Lib "apigid32.dll" Alias _
"agGetAddressForObject" (vbstring As String) As Long
```

All of these aliases call a very simple function that returns as a Long value the parameter that was passed. It can be useful in determining the value placed on the top of a stack for different parameters. It can also be used to retrieve the address of a variable when it is passed by reference, a task that is more frequently handled now using the VarPtr operator.

agGetStringFrom2NullBuffer

```
Declare Function agGetStringFrom2NullBuffer Lib "apigid32.dll" (ByVal ptr As _
Long) As String
```

There are a number of API functions that load a buffer with a series of strings, where each string is separated from the next by a NULL character and the final string is followed by two NULL characters. Loading a buffer of this type into a Visual Basic string is possible using VB and API functions alone, but it is a complex task that includes using API functions to calculate the length of each string and to copy each string individually. This function takes as a parameter a pointer to a memory buffer containing a double NULL-terminated set of strings, and returns a VB string with all of the strings in a single string (still separated by NULL characters with a double NULL termination at the end). You can then parse the individual strings easily using the VB Instr and Mid$ functions.

agGetStringFromPointer

```
Declare Function agGetStringFromPointer Lib "apigid32.dll" Alias _
"agGetStringFromLPSTR" (ByVal ptr As Long) As String
```

This function takes a parameter containing a memory pointer to a NULL-terminated ANSI string and returns a Visual Basic string containing the string (without the NULL terminating character). This function is the easiest way to convert a pointer to a NULL-terminated string into a Visual Basic string.

FileTime Functions

A number of API functions use 64-bit arithmetic to handle very large numeric variables such as dates, times, and sizes of files or disk drives. Visual Basic provides no support for 64-bit arithmetic, and it can be difficult to handle given that VB does not have an unsigned 32-bit data type. The following functions provide 64-bit arithmetic operations using structures that contain two 32-bit values. The FILETIME and LARGE_INTEGER structures are examples of structures that will work with these functions.

agAddFileTimes

```
Declare Sub agAddFileTimes Lib "apigid32.dll" (f1 As Any, f2 As Any, f3 As Any)
```

This function adds the contents of one FILETIME structure to another. It can also be used with LARGE_INTEGER and other 64-bit integer-based structures. The sum f1 and f2 is loaded into f3.

agConvertDoubleToFileTime

```
Declare Sub agConvertDoubleToFileTime Lib "apigid32.dll" (ByVal d As Double, f1 _
As Any)
```

This function loads the contents of a FILETIME structure from a floating point value. It can also be used with LARGE_INTEGER and other 64-bit integer-based structures.

agConvertFileTimeToDouble

```
Declare Function agConvertFileTimeToDouble Lib "apigid32.dll" (f1 As Any) As
Double
```

This function returns the contents of a FILETIME structure as a floating point value. It can also be used with LARGE_INTEGER and other 64-bit integer-based structures.

agNegateFileTimes

```
Declare Sub agNegateFileTime Lib "apigid32.dll" (f1 As Any)
```

This function negates the contents of one FILETIME structure from another. It can also be used with LARGE_INTEGER and other 64-bit integer-based structures. After this call, f1 will be equal to $-f1$.

agSubtractFileTimes

```
Declare Sub agSubtractFileTimes Lib "apigid32.dll" (f1 As Any, f2 As Any, f3 As
Any)
```

This function subtracts the contents of one FILETIME structure from another. It can also be used with LARGE_INTEGER and other 64-bit integer-based structures. After this call, f3 will be equal to $f1-f2$.

Miscellaneous

This function doesn't fit into any of the previous categories.

agIsValidName

```
Declare Function agIsValidName Lib "apigid32.dll" (ByVal o As Object, _
ByVal lpname As String) As Long
```

Given an object reference in parameter o, this function will return True (non-zero) if the string in the lpname parameter represents a method or property name for the automation interface of the object.

Index

D

G

H

I

J

K

L